Geoffrey Bell

The Protestants of Ulster

Second impression 1978
Third impression 1982
First published 1976 by Pluto Press Limited
Unit 10 Spencer Court, 7 Chalcot Road, London NW1 8LH
Copyright © Pluto Press 1976
ISBN 0 904383 08 3
Printed and bound in Great Britain by
The Camelot Press Limited, Southampton
Cover picture: Camera Press Limited
Cover designed by Richard Hollis, GrR

Contents

Acknowledgements / vi
Introduction / vii

1. 'This we will maintain' / 1
2. Ancient Privileges / 15
3. Leaders of the Cause / 34
4. The Protestant Way of Life / 48
5. Lundies / 64
6. The Workers / 80
7. The Bosses / 93
8. The Fenians / 106
9. Protestantism's Last Stand / 119
10. 'O God our help in ages past,
    Our hope for years to come' / 132

References / 145
Index / 155

Acknowledgements

Many people have helped me in many ways with this book. I would give special mention to Jimmy Grealy, Michael Kidron, Mary Margaret McHugh, Liz Stewart, and especially Jim Smyth of Queens University, Belfast.

I also thank those who work in the Linen Hall Library, Belfast, the British Museum Newspaper Library at Colindale and the library of the London School of Economics.

This book is for my parents in appreciation for allowing me to think for myself. No mean feat in Belfast.

Geoffrey Bell
Belfast 1972
London 1976

Introduction

The Protestants of Northern Ireland are the most misunderstood and criticised community in western Europe. They do not deserve to be misunderstood; this book explores whether they deserve to be criticised.

1

'This We Will Maintain'

On Sunday, 30 January 1972, a demonstration took place on the streets of Derry City, Northern Ireland. The march was in protest at the continuing internment, without trial or release date, of hundreds of men in the six north-eastern counties of Ireland. Internment broke no new fresh ground. It had been used many, many times in the centuries during which England had tried to rule her oldest and most restless dominion. That it needed to be invoked again in the 1970s was a reflection of past failures, past over-reactions; most of all it was a testament to the perennial nature of England's 'Irish Problem'. Derry was an appropriate venue for the demonstration. The city had the highest rate of unemployment in the United Kingdom. It had witnessed on 5 October 1968 the start of the latest round in the Irish question when a small civil rights march was batonned to the ground by the forces of law and order. It was where, in the summer of 1969, British troops had for the first time in many years stepped onto the streets of Ireland. And, on 30 January 1972, it was again Derry City which became the centre of the political, historical and emotional stage when those same troops shot dead fourteen demonstrators.

Afterwards there were attempts to explain, to justify. Reginald Maudling, the British Home Secretary excused the soldiers in parliament; the English Chief Justice, in a subsequent inquiry, exonerated the troops. This was hardly surprising, and, for those who had reached the conclusion that the despoilers of Ireland were not individual kings, individual prime ministers, individual soldiers or individual factory-owners, this was the final proof of the collective guilt of the British establishment. But, like most other things that establishment had done in Ireland, the whitewash failed.

1

There were too many independent witnesses, there was too much evidence, too much blood for the British version to be sustained. The truth, fourteen innocent victims, emerged and was accepted by the rest of the world and, three years later, was even grudgingly accepted by the British government when the families of the victims were given compensation, pittance though it was. 'Bloody Sunday' it came to be called, naturally and without pretension. A title of disgrace for the perpetrators, a title of anger for the victims' community. There was no pride in Bloody Sunday.

Correction; there was:

Bloody Sunday

Sunday morning went for a drive,
Took along my colt 45.
Hey, Hey, Hey, what a beautiful day.
Went to Derry not on a hunch,
Knew I'd get a taig* before lunch,
Hey, Hey, Hey, it's a beautiful day.

Taigs were marching like on the Falls,
I opened up from Derry's Walls,
Hey, Hey, Hey, what a beautiful day.
Taigs to army said it was you,
Didn't know I was there too,
Hey, Hey, Hey, it's a beautiful day.

Chorus

Bang, Bang, Bang, Bloody Sunday,
This is my, my, my, beautiful day,
When I say, say, say, Bloody Sunday,
I mean my, oh, my,
What a beautiful day.[1]

There is no truth in the claim that civilians participated in the Derry murders, but the song was not composed from any desire for

* Taig – Catholic.

2

factual accuracy. The song was composed as a celebration for what happened; literally, something to sing about. The words were written by someone who describes himself as a 'UDA detainee', that is a member of the largest contemporary Protestant private army, the Ulster Defence Association, someone who, like those the Derry dead were demonstrating for, was detained or interned without trial. The words appear in a songbook published by the UDA in 1974. So while the lyrics could be dismissed as the product of a diseased mind the sentiments they express are paraded for approval by an organisation which represents a considerable section of the Protestant community in Northern Ireland.

With such songs as their popular expression it is not surprising that the Protestants of Northern Ireland should have few friends or that they are 'scorned by all the world' as another recent Belfast Protestant song puts it.[2] Certainly the days have long gone when the British press rushed to publicise the opinions and causes of the Northern Ireland Catholics – the British army has become involved since – but while that press now distorts, lies about or, more commonly, disregards what is happening in Northern Ireland, and while the Catholics of Derry, Belfast and elsewhere are now branded as murderers, terrorists, animals, the full circle has not been completed. The Protestants have not replaced the poor downtrodden Catholics in the fawning patronage of the world outside the six north-eastern counties of Ireland. Protestant Ulster remains, in the words of another of its songsters, 'Maligned and degraded, her ills over-rated.'[3] To which the spectator might reply that it is rather difficult to over-rate the ills of Protestant Ulster.

For the community's inhabitants that would be just one more of the many slanders they have had to suffer; it is the world which has judged Protestant Ulster wrong, not Protestant Ulster which errs. There is, there has to be, a conspiracy. As the Ulster Unionist Party which controlled the government of Northern Ireland from 1921 until 1972 put it, Northern Ireland has been subject to 'a vicious and insidious campaign which colours the reports and commentaries of even the most impeccable and reliable observers.'[4]

So Ulster has few friends. Of course it is only to be expected that the international conspiracy of the left has rushed to adopt the Irish Catholics, that atheist extremists label the Protestants of Northern Ireland reactionary or even fascist. But what of the others? What of Harold Wilson, a spokesman if ever there was of plodding British respectability, how is Harold Wilson to be explained when in a television broadcast in May 1974 he called the Protestants 'people who spend their lives sponging on Westminster and on British democracy'? The conspiracy embraces them all.

Some have swum against the tide of abuse and denigration. Enoch Powell, who made his name pointing out black skins in England, has offered himself as an ally. The National Front, the English fascist party, has held demonstrations in London in support of the Ulster Protestants. Even a few members of the 'marxist' left in Ireland, exponents of a 'Two Nations' theory have attempted to explain to the Protestants that, on Stalin's definition of nationality, they have every right to do what they are doing. Even Joseph Stalin hardly deserves that.

Such friends have been of little benefit to the Protestant cause, and have not stopped the Protestants from withdrawing further into themselves. When Wilson called them spongers, they pinned sponges on their lapels as a token of their attitude to him. Presumably to be insulted by that gentleman could be taken as a compliment. The sponge-wearing was more than that; it was a gesture of defiance to a British government that apparently no longer wanted to know; it was a message to the leader of that government:

> Who do you think you are kidding Mr Wilson
> If you think old Ulster's done.[5]

Temporary though the victory was, the sponge-wearers and the Protestant songsters won. In May 1974 they destroyed the

British establishment's plans for Northern Ireland. The Protestants had been instructed to share power with Catholics; the Protestants went on strike. They had been told that their Northern Ireland had to take its place in a Council of Ireland, powerless though that Council was to be; the Protestants went on strike. The British government sent over the General Secretary of the British Trade Union Congress to lead a march to break the strike; the march was a fiasco, the strike accelerated. Finally the government surrendered. The Sunningdale Agreement, which had encompassed power-sharing and the Council of Ireland was, like so many British plans before, laid to rest. The Northern Ireland Executive, made up of politicians who had supported Sunningdale, collapsed. The spongers won.

The night of the victory, 28 May, was for the Protestants of Ulster, the 'loyalists' as they had come to be known, a night of celebration. It scarcely mattered that the traditional foe of those loyalists, the Irish Republican Army, were as pleased as they were about the collapse of Sunningdale. It scarcely mattered that a greater victory, the downfall of the Northern Ireland parliament, had been gained by the IRA more than two years earlier, just six weeks after Bloody Sunday. If it did matter no one would care to mention it as the bonfires raged, as the old Protestant songs were sung, as they remembered victories past, when – to quote one of the leading political parties – 'The loyalists were prepared to defy and did defy the Westminister government'.[6]

In Ireland there is nothing unusual in seeking inspiration from the past. History lives in Ireland like nowhere else, not because the whole Irish race is somehow trapped in it, but because the consequences of that past are a living reality and cannot be wished away. The 'settlement' of the Irish problem in the years 1912–21 is difficult to ignore because that settlement settled nothing. So let us begin with those years, with the establishment of the political state of Protestant Ulster.

In 1921 no organised grouping in Ireland, Protestant or Catholic, loyalist or republican, sought the establishment of a separate Northern Ireland. The nationalists and republicans had sought to secure a 32-county Ireland. There were disagreements, and there was to be a civil war over the degree of independence that Ireland should gain from England, there were different degrees of emphasis on the necessity of keeping Ireland undivided, and although many on the nationalist side were naïvely willing to agree to partition as a temporary expedient, nobody accepted the principle of a divided Ireland.

On the loyalist side, too, partition was never mentioned as a negotiating aim. The great Unionist declaration, the 1912 Ulster Covenant signed by 471,414 people, spoke of 'using all means which may be found necessary to defeat the present conspiracy to set up a Home Rule parliament in Ireland'.[7] There was no mention of a separate Ulster settlement, or of allowing a portion of Ireland to be granted Home Rule. The Unionist opposition, in theory at any rate, was opposed to any form of Home Rule Ireland. The thousands who signed the Ulster Covenant were, in effect, signing for the continuation of what has now become the loyalists' abomination, direct rule from Westminster; but the direct rule they were asking for was to apply to all of Ireland, not just to part of it.

The partition of Ireland, the establishment of two separate Home Rule parliaments, one in the north and one in the south, was a compromise suggested by the British government. After two years of guerilla fighting it was reluctantly accepted by the nationalists on the unwritten understanding, reached with the British Prime Minister, Lloyd George, that it would be temporary. The Unionists accepted partition as the best they could get and as a means of avoiding democratic control over the six north-eastern counties by all the Irish people. The Unionists never made any pretence that the establishment of the Northern Ireland parliament was a satisfactory outcome. They never claimed that the six counties which came under the rule of that parliament had a natural boundary.

Historically and geographically Ulster consisted of nine counties and accepting six was, for the Unionists, a matter of convenience. As Lord Cushendon, one of the leaders of Ulster Unionism at the time said,

> To separate themselves from fellow loyalists in Monaghan, Cavan and Donegal was hateful to every delegate from the other six counties . . . but the inextricable index of statistics demonstrated that although Unionists were in a majority when geographical Ulster was considered as a unit, yet the distribution of population made it certain that a separate parliament for the whole province would have a precarious existence, while its administration of purely nationalist districts would mean unending conflict.[8]

So the boundaries of the 'Ulster' state were ratified by the Unionists because they were guaranteed a permanent majority within those boundaries.

Even unplanned children have parents, and the history of Protestant loyalism does not begin with the establishment of the Northern Ireland state. For all the artificialities of partition it did recognise a certain reality – the majority of the Protestants of north-east Ireland were adamant in their opposition to Irish self-determination. This reflected one of the few successes a British administration has ever had in Ireland – the plantation in the seventeenth century of Scottish and English settlers, who were Protestant, in an Ulster which until then had been the most rebellious of the four Irish provinces. Let a traditional loyalist song take up the story:

> Where flows the Mersey to the sea,
> Came they who wield the spear,
> And some from Clyde's fair banks sailed forth,
> Whose only scoff was fear,
> Their left hand held the bull-hide targe,
> The right the broad claymore,
> And soon fair Ulster knew their names,
> From Foyle to Lough Neagh's shore.
>
> They won fair Ulster by the sword,
> By toil they keep it now,

And can'st fair Albion boast,
A gem more fair upon the brow?
And when Ben Moore from o'er the deep,
On Killeshandra's lakes,
Our fathers won the Celtic soil,
We'll keep it for their sakes.[9]

A colonists' song, but the years seem distant when the colonists and those in whose name they came have sung such songs in unison. Now the loyalists of north-east Ireland have become an embarrassment to all but themselves; 'spongers' as Harold Wilson called them. 'What a bloody awful country', exclaimed Reginald Maudling when Home Secretary, as he ordered a large Scotch on the plane from Belfast.[10]

So there is the first and most obvious paradox: a community which was planted and nurtured by the rulers of Britain, a community which blazens its loyalty to Britain, but which both in the past, in 1912 when the loyalists pledged themselves to defy the British parliament, and today, as Ulster flags replace Union Jacks on the streets of Northern Ireland, a community whose loyalism appears a moveable feast; a cause of much head-scratching among those of whom the loyalists claim to be part. There is another side to the paradox: a mother country which no longer understands its carefully bred offspring; which imposed a parliament against the wishes of its truculent Ulster sons; which took it away again in 1972 while the ungrateful sons who never knew what was good for them in the first place were demanding it back.

The relationship between the heart of the Empire and part of that empire is certainly unconventional, and the loyalists too scratch their heads and wonder what it is all about:

For being British we have had the privilege to lose our democratically elected local government, thus putting us in a state of limbo which Westiminster cannot cope with, never mind understand ... we are enforced to have to sit and watch every Tom, Dick and Harry of English politicians taking notes and talking a lot

8

of rubbish about our troubles. . . . The privilege of being British means having to sit back and watch people whom you know have no love for this country being taken by the hand by blind politicians grasping for an answer to our troubles. The loyalist people have certainly paid a heavy price for the privilege of being British . . . our sacrifices in two world wars and our service to Britain count for nothing when the chips are down. We are being used in a dirty political game by those whom we depend on. Yes the privilege of being British falls heavily on Ulstermen's shoulders and only time will tell how long we can carry the burden.[11]

There speaks the most popular contemporary loyalist newspaper, edited by one John McKeague, who said on a British televison programme after 30 January 1972, 'What we need are one, two, three, many more Bloody Sundays.' The voice of unreason, the voice of illogicality, a Britishness which is a thousand miles away from the self-proclaimed reasonableness, tolerance and gradualism of the true British.

Fortunately or unfortunately, British home secretaries cannot wash away their guilt with a large Scotch on a plane from Belfast. Randolph Churchill it was, who coined the now immortal words from the loyalists' bumper book of clichés, 'Ulster Will Fight and Ulster Will be Right'; and it was Churchill's party leader, Lord Salisbury, who wrote last century: 'On Tory principles the case presents much that is painful, but no perplexity whatever. Ireland must be kept, by persuasion if possible, if not by force.'[12] Carrying on this tradition, another Tory prime minister, Bonar Law, said when backing the Ulster loyalists' stand of 1912: 'We shall not be guided by the considerations, we shall not be restrained by the bonds which would influence our action in any ordinary political struggle. We shall use whatever means seem most likely to be effective.'[13]

The London politicians of today may tut-tut and lecture against such sentiments but the Protestants of Ulster cannot so comfortably forget their traditions or smugly brush aside their past. Another song, written around the time Bonar Law and his colleagues were urging illegal resistance to the Westminster parliament, sums up what Protestants had been led to believe and expect for many years:

> Then rally Ulster's loyal sons,
> And proud your banners wave,
> With heart and voice make it your choice,
> Our blood-bought rights to save,
> Our brethren across the sea,
> Will join the glad refrain,
> Then in God's name your watchword raise,
> The Union We'll Maintain.[14]

'The Union We'll Maintain' has become another loyalist catch phrase, handed down from Orange father to Orange son, as if it were a religious commandment. The more common abbreviated version, 'This We Will Maintain' is still to be found daubed on the walls of working-class Befast, walls which enclose some of the worst slums in the British Isles. 'This We Will Maintain' refers to the Union and not to the crumbling tenements, although the connection between the two is more than accidental.

Therein lies the second paradox. The broken-down houses of Belfast are just one manifestation of the social and economic conditions that city has been made to suffer since its birth as the industrial capital of Ireland. There are many others: high unemployment, low wages, overcrowding. And yet the message broadcast by the working-class Protestants who live there is a message of conservatism. Not simply the sloganising symbolism of 'This We Will Maintain' but also an allegiance to the Ulster Unionist Party which, until very recently, was an ally of the British Tories but which outdid even their record of upper-class abundance and lower-class deprivation. What a paradox – a majority of the inhabitants of the most depressed region in the United Kingdom shouting louder than any others of their allegiance to that polity. The paradox of a Unionist Party enjoying uninterrupted government for over fifty years yet with a social and economic record which by all normal rules of political behaviour would have resulted in that party's cremation a long time ago. Even now when at last many lower-class Protestants have started to question the establishment party, their challenge is not a reaction against the slums and dole queues but a protest against their party's tinkering with the traditions and methods of the old days. It is an attack from the right, a plea for times past.

This leads to the third paradox, symbolised by the Ulster Workers' Council General Strike of May 1974, the only successful general strike in the long history of the United Kingdom. The paradox lies not in the rarity of the UWC strike, rather it is in its nature. All the textbooks tell us that a general strike is concerned with advancing the cause of a more equal society, is aimed at democratising not just the politics but society and economic life as well. Yet the UWC strike aimed at stopping a greater sharing of power, at preventing a greater degree of co-operation among the divided Irish population. For the first time since the foundation of the Northern Ireland state the Protestant working class exercised power – to maintain working-class division, in support of the status quo.

By all normal standards the behaviour of the Protestants of Northern Ireland is peculiar. It is tempting to dismiss them with a shrug of the shoulders and to explain the situation in Northern Ireland with a deprecating 'They're Irish of course' – not quite the effect the Ulster Protestants hope for, but general enough. Harold Wilson's cheap rhetoric speaks volumes: 'Loyalist is used to describe people who have no scruples about firing on British troops and who defy every principle of law and order which decent people in the United Kingdom hold dear.'[15] There it is, bluntly and without shame. The loyalists are not 'decent people'. Problem solved.

There have been other more considered theories. The Vanguard Party whose former leader, William Craig, was one of the most popular politicians within the Northern Ireland Protestant community, explained the gulf between the loyalists and the British in this fashion:

> Two different communities in Great Britain and Ulster at different stages of development by virtue of different historical experiences possess different scales of reference by which to measure, weigh and judge. The cardinal error is for one to judge events in the other by its different value system ... British weakness for transplanting their own value categories explains what Ulster people mean when they say that the British are incapable of understanding Ulster problems.[16]

This is not the first time the Empire's insistence on exporting its version of civilisation to the colonies has been questioned. There are many outside the borders of England's green and pleasant land who would testify to the self-righteousness of official British attitudes. The problem here is not in the acknowledgement of differences in culture and outlook between Ulster and Britain but in the setting in which the quotation appears. Just four paragraphs later, the Vanguard Party continues:

> The loyalist cause in Ulster is the preservation of a British tradition and heritage within which and only within which can the loyalist community live and breathe and have its being ... what is at stake is the maintenance of that distinct way of life and culture.[17]

No training in logic is necessary to detect the contradiction between the two statements – we object to Britain forcing its way of life and way of thinking on us, but we'll fight to the death to keep them. But then, as another loyalist put it, 'We are not good at propaganda and are not good at extolling our virtues.'[18]

Another popular theory explains the Northern Ireland conflict in terms of religion. 'A seventeenth-century religious war' is turned out so often by politicians and editorial-writers that it needs no accrediting. It is a convenient description and one for which the loyalist cause seems only too happy to provide evidence. Songs such as the following appear to suggest a mind locked in the mythology of the crusades, let alone the seventeenth century:

> Are you arming Brother Protestants,
> Are you arming for the fray,

Are you resolved on victory,
And crushing Papal sway,
And do you dare, in solemn trust,
Upon the King of kings,
To fight your battles underneath,
The shadow of his wings?[19]

Religion certainly plays a large part in the culture and ideology of many Protestants in Northern Ireland. It is used as an easily available means of recognition. But the ancestors of the present-day loyalists were planted not to convert Ireland to Protestantism, but to hold Ireland for England. If, to use another example, a favourite with Unionist propagandists, many Protestants left or were driven out of the twenty-six counties after partition, it was not because they attended or didn't attend a certain church, but because they were usually the largest landowners and the strongest in their support of the imperial connection. As such they were in opposition to, and felt uncomfortable with, the prevailing republican ideology. Religious affiliation is merely a manifestation of the divisions in Ireland, not its cause. Protestantism is only one of the characteristics of the loyalist community. A renewal of the campaign for the dissolution of the monasteries was not among the UWC demands.

The obvious truism that there are two communities in Northern Ireland has led to a further explanation of what the loyalists are about – the Two Nations theory, which postulates irreconcilable differences between the 'Protestant nation' and the 'Catholic nation' in Ireland, a difference expressed in the existence of two separate states. Since these differences are natural, claim the Two Nations advocates, the Protestants have the right to maintain their 'nation', that is the Northern Ireland state, and to rule it as they will. This theory was first propounded by the British and Irish Communist Organisation (B & ICO), which previously had distinguished itself by rallying to the defence of Stalin's memory when Krushchev denounced him. It has received the patronage, in one form or another, of such worthy figures as Dr Conor Cruise O'Brien, author, diplomat, historian and an Irish Labour Party member of the Irish coalition government. In Ulster itself the theory has the support of the Vanguard Party, whose proudest publication is entitled *Ulster, A Nation*, as well as the blessings of various loyalist community newspapers.

The Two Nations theory is the other side of Harold Wilson's 'not decent people' coin – not only are the Protestants 'decent' but their political expression, Ulster Unionism, is a sanctified cause. With such conclusions the Two Nations theory, like the religious war theory or the Harold Wilson theory, seems to offer an easy way out of the Protestant enigma. But like the other theories it raises more problems than it solves. It cannot explain, for example, why the republican wing of the so-called 'Catholic nation' has been as uncompromisingly opposed to successive governments of the twenty-six counties, as it has been to the governments of the supposed 'Protestant nation'. It cannot explain how Brian Faulkner, Northern Ireland's last Prime Minister could unite with the Irish Prime Minister, Liam Cosgrave, in accepting a Council of Ireland and in banning the Provisional IRA. Or how Conor Cruise O'Brien, a leading representative of the dreaded 'Catholic nation', can have more in common with the B & ICO than he has with his fellow 'Catholic nationalists', the Provisionals.

The Protestants of Northern Ireland appear impervious to theories and explanations. They remain suspicious and hostile of anyone not of their community. And the sign on the wall still reads, 'This We Will Maintain'.

2

Ancient Privileges

At the end of the eighteenth century, when the United Irishmen were preparing to stage a revolt against the British Empire, General Lake, who was in charge of suppressing the rebellious natives in the north of Ireland was informed by another general under his command:

> I have arranged . . . to increase the animosity between Orangemen and the United Irish. Upon that animosity depends the safety of the centre counties of the north. Were the Orangemen disarmed or put down or were they coalesced with the other party, the whole of Ulster would be as bad as Antrim and Down.[1]

General Lake had good reason to commend his henchman's tactic. In the 1790s the animosity between Protestants and Catholics was a good deal less than at any time before or since. Northern Irish Presbyterians had become a strong influence in the United Irishmen and many were looking towards self-government as a political programme. In part this sprang from the restrictions they themselves had suffered under the British government's sectarian policies, which were designed to suppress all signs of unorthodoxy; in part it was because the Presbyterian gentry and mercantile classes had come to recognise that the trading and commercial relationship which the British imposed on Ireland restricted their economic advancement. At a more general level the Presbyterian middle classes, like the middle classes in the United States and France, were part of a general movement advancing the cause of equality. Whatever the reason, the possibility that the always disaffected Catholics and a section, albeit a minority, of the Protestants might come together had General Lake and those whom he represented in Ireland apply more vigorously than ever before the age-old policy of divide and rule.

Although many Presbyterians took part in the United Irishmen Rising of 1798, the government succeeded. Ireland was saved for England by encouraging Protestant sectarianism, by mercilessly putting down the republicans before and during the rising and by assisting in the hostility between the Catholic and Protestant peasantry. Within two years of the rising's defeat, the Act of Union was passed giving Westminster direct authority over Ireland.

The 1798 Rebellion and the involvement of Ulster Protestants in that rebellion have been a romantic inspiration for Irish republicans ever since, especially as there has been no comparable unity since then. Many of the Protestants who took part in the radical nationalist movement of the late eighteenth century emigrated to America; others were victims of General Lake's repression. But a more substantial reason for the Protestant Irish never returning to the Irish nationalist fold was the economic development of Ireland in the nineteenth century. Through that development the divisions between the two communities was strengthened and cemented and their economic interests were made to differ. Irish economic history is a much neglected field for study and although this book will do little to rectify the situation it is important at the outset to lift Irish history out of the realms of religious mysticism and cultural affiliations.

One material aspect existed before the nineteenth century – the differences in land tenure between Ulster and the three other provinces of Ireland. The 'Ulster Custom' gave more security to tenants in Ulster than those elsewhere and, although the differences had lessened by the end of the nineteenth century, a more general series of differentials emerged; Ulster became relatively richer as Belfast grew to become the industrial capital of Ireland. Table 2.1 shows that in 1891 Ireland as a whole suffered a higher rate of officially-defined pauperism than Great Britain, but Belfast did not: its rate was below the English, Welsh and Scottish average, and lower than every other major city except Birmingham. In the Irish

16

2.1 Level of Pauperism, Britain and Ireland, 1891

	rate per 1,000		rate per 1,000
England and Wales	197	London	215
Scotland	180	Newcastle	191
Ireland	245	Bolton	147
		Manchester	159
		Liverpool	194
		Birmingham	103
		Bristol	311
		Glasgow	203
		Dublin	226
		Cork, Waterford and Limerick	437
		Belfast	110
		Galway	181

Data: UK Labour Gazette, June 1893

context Belfast shines out like a beacon. Tables 2.2 and 2.3 qualify this first picture slightly and illustrate that, at least in the building and linen trades, while skilled workmen in Belfast tended to be no worse off and in some instances better off, in terms of wage rates, than their British counterparts, the same did not apply to unskilled workers. Labourers in Belfast were at the very bottom of the wages league.

The tables imply that there was a greater difference in wages between the 'labour aristocracy' and the rest of the working class in Belfast than in the towns of Britain. Further evidence of the similarity in skilled wage rates in Belfast and Britain is given in table 2.4, which also shows that rates were a good deal better in Belfast than elsewhere in Ireland. Of course wage rates are not the only indication of living standards but in this respect it is interesting to note that rents in Dublin at the time were higher than they were in Belfast,[2] so the differences in wage rates in the two cities

2.2 Weekly Wage Rates in Building Trades, 1891

	bricklayer	carpenter	plasterer	plumber	painter	bricklayers' labourer	plasterers' labourer
shillings and pence							
London	39.5	39.5	39.5	39.2	36.1	26.3	26.3
SW England and Cardiff	31.4	30.7	32.5	32.5	27.0	19.8	19.11
Midlands	34.2	32.10	33.9	33.9	31.0	21.8	22.6
England, E. counties	28.1	29.11	34.0	31.5	27.2	16.8	16.8
Lancashire	37.8	34.5	34.4	35.0	32.3	24.8	24.3
Yorkshire	32.9	29.11	31.9	31.10	29.2	22.1	22.5
England, N. counties	33.0	31.5	31.11	32.7	30.10	21.3	21.8
Scotland	35.8	27.10	29.3	28.8	30.10	21.1	21.1
Belfast	36.0	33.9	33.3	36.0	33.9	16.0	16.0

Data: British Parliamentary Papers, 1893, vol.83, pt.2

2.3 Weekly Wage Rates in the Linen Industry, 1886

	rougher	tenter and turner	head warehouse-man	yarn storeman	gate-keeper	labourer
shillings and pence						
Belfast	18.6	37.6	31.6	17.0	15.2	13.2
Ulster (excl. Belfast)	16.8	30.5	37.11	13.5	12.5	9.10
Scotland	18.7	23.11	29.10	19.6	17.6	16.2
West Riding	19.4	26.5	30.10	21.0	19.8	17.8

Data: British Parliamentary Papers, 1899, vol.70

2.4 Weekly Wage Rates in Engineering, 1896

	platers (heavy)		platers (light)		riveters	
	B*	S†	B	S	B	S
	shillings and pence					
Belfast	41.0	39.6	41.0	39.0	35.6	35.0
Dublin	36.0	36.0	36.0	36.0	32.0	32.0
Cardiff	43.0	42.0	43.0	42.0	42.0	39.0
Sunderland	41.0	39.6	39.0	36.6	37.6	34.6
Hull	39.0	39.0	39.0	39.0	34.0	34.0
Liverpool	42.0	40.6	40.0	38.6	36.6	34.6
	* B = boilershops			† S = shipyards		

Data: *British Parliamentary Papers, 1897, vol.84*

understated the real differences in spending power. The regional variation in Irish wage rates is further illustrated in table 2.5, which gives the wages of female domestic servants. There is a good deal of other evidence which suggests that conditions in Ulster, and Belfast in particular, were better than elsewhere in Ireland. For example, the annual death rate in Belfast at 23·8 per cent was lower than in Dublin at 27·5 per cent;[3] the numbers applying for outdoor relief was much lower in Ulster than elsewhere (see table 2.6). Clearly there was a further 'labour aristocracy', definable in terms of geography.

There is a third and equally important labour aristocracy, in Ulster itself, definable in terms of religion. The 1891 Irish census showed that 5,008 out of the 8,900 in workhouses that year were Catholics, or 55 per cent, compared with the 46 per cent of Catholics in the Ulster population as a whole. These figures probably underestimate the differences, as more Catholics lived in rural areas where there were fewer workhouses. A further

2.5 Average Monthly Wages of Female
Domestic Servants, 1898

| | Number of servants employed in household | | | |
	one	two	three	four
	pounds and shillings			
Belfast	12.6	13.9	16.7	17.1
Dublin	10.8	13.5	15.3	16.6
Cork and				
Limerick	9.5	11.1	13.9	14.7

*Data: British Parliamentary Papers (Irish Univer-
sity Press edition, vol.20: Industrial Relations)*

2.6 Number of People
Receiving Outdoor Relief

	1881 one in	1891 one in
Leinster	54	61
Munster	54	43
Connaught	88	80
Ulster	278	224

Data: 1891 census, Ireland

indication is to be found in the illiteracy rates; obviously it tended to
be the poorest who could neither read nor write. Table 2.7 gives a
breakdown of illiteracy by religion in selected Ulster counties and
in Belfast. But the clearest illustration of the differences within the
Belfast working class is provided by the breakdown of jobs and

2.7 Illiteracy in Ulster by Religion, 1891 and 1901

	Catholic	Episcopalian	Presbyterian	Methodist
	per cent			
1891				
Monaghan	21·9	8·5	4·9	3·7
Antrim	15·8	10·8	5·3	4·7
Armagh	26·8	15·3	6·1	6·1
Tyrone	23·4	13·5	7·0	4·4
Down	21·2	10·5	5·5	5·1
1901				
Belfast	12·2	8·4	4·8	4·6

Data: census, 1891 and 1901, Ireland

professions by religious affiliation. Table 2.8 illustrates the position in 1901.

From table 2.8 it is clear that Catholics were under-represented in the professions, such as accountancy, and in middle class employment, such as in insurance and banks. Equally significant, they were under-represented in the skilled working-class jobs and over-represented in domestic service. There is an interesting contrast between employment in the civil service and in local government. Male Catholic workers in the civil service were actually over-represented while in local government the reverse applied, suggesting that discrimination did not apply where the central Westminster government exercised control but that where the local Unionists did, Catholics were at a marked disadvantage.

So by the end of the nineteenth century what privileges there were in Ireland were enjoyed by the Protestant community. The main area of Protestant concentration in Ireland, the north-east, had a higher standard of living, comparable at some levels to that in Britain. Within the north-east the middle and upper classes were

2.8 Religious Affiliation in Selected Jobs, Belfast, 1901

	Total Catholics			Total Catholics	
	no.	per cent		no.	per cent
Civil service			Barristers and		
men	471	28·3	solicitors	175	22·28
women	159	23·37	Doctors	218	7·34
Local government			Bank employees	275	6·18
men	274	8·39	Carpenters and		
women	128	17·18	joiners	3,974	15·55
Accountants			Plumbers	830	11·56
men	307	10·75	Millwrights	54	5·55
women	22	13·63	Engine and		
Domestic servants			machine makers	631	9·98
men	285	30·52	Fitters and turners	1,721	11·15
women	7,556	42·15	Dentists	80	16·25
Catholics as percentage of			Merchants	134	8·21
population: 24·3			Insurance		
			employees	274	8·39

Data: 1901 census, Ireland

overwhelmingly Protestant. Within the lower classes, Protestants were over-represented in the higher-paid and Catholics in the lower-paid jobs, and the pay differential between the jobs was greater than in Britain, producing a further widening of the economic gap between Catholic and Protestant workers. The political effect of such differences hardly needs spelling out. The marginally privileged Protestants, working-class and others, were aware that they were not at the bottom of the economic heap. They feared any political change which would give the majority population, the Catholics, a greater influence in running the country and open the minority's privileges to challenge. Although social and economic differences were not the only factors working on the consciousness of the Protestant working class they did a great deal to prevent the Protestant workers from seeing any benefit to themselves from working-class unity. Their position was different from that of the Catholic workers and it was a difference they recognised.

A meeting of Protestant trade unionists held in Belfast in 1914 articulated their opposition to Home Rule for Ireland. It was argued that labour laws would be less progressive in a Home Rule Ireland than in Britain, that conditions in Belfast were better than in Dublin, that Home Rule would put power into the hands of farmers, that the material benefits of living in Belfast would be lost under Home Rule. Many of the trade unionists at the meeting recognised that they were speaking in the interests of a minority amongst workers. One speaker declared that he was 'A Protestant, a Unionist and a (Ulster) Volunteer'; another, 'that as trade unionists we do not pretend to speak for Catholic trade unionists'. The same speaker went on to state the essence of the Protestant workers' case:

> The only reason why the nationalists supported Home Rule was because they would have a dominating power, a power which would enable them to fill every public office with men of their own way of thinking. That was the motive which lay at the back of the Home Rule sentiment – it represented the advance of Roman Catholicism.[4]

In short what the Protestant workers were saying was that they feared self-determination because it would mean majority rule and probably majority benefit; what was defended was minority rule and, as the Protestant workers saw it, minority benefit.

The Protestant workers, led and controlled by the Protestant upper class, were successful. Partition left the Protestants in control of their own house. Although the effective power of the Northern Ireland government established in 1921 was limited overall, as far as internal policies were concerned it was wide-ranging. Just one example should do. In 1935 nine people were killed in an attempted pogrom against Catholics, but when the matter was raised in the Westminster House of Commons, Stanley Baldwin, the Prime Minister of the day, replied that the riots were solely a matter for the Northern Ireland government and could not be discussed at Westminster. And that was Westminster's characteristic response until August 1969, when the blood flowed too freely and openly to be comfortably ignored. A Northern Ireland in which a divided working class was a quiescent working class was allowed to go its own way.

The consequences of unfettered Unionist control were bleak. One indication is provided in table 2.9, which compares the level of unemployment in Northern Ireland and Britain during the inter-war years, and illustrates the differences which now separated the conditions of the workers in the two areas. Obviously the Northern Ireland government cannot be held responsible for the acute

2.9 Unemployment, 1922–38, Northern Ireland and Great Britain

	NI	GB		NI	GB		NI	GB
	per cent							
1922	22·9	14·1	1928	17·2	10·7	1934	23·9	16·6
1923	17·9	11·6	1929	15·1	10·3	1935	25·3	15·3
1924	16·6	10·2	1930	24·3	15·8	1936	23·1	13·0
1925	24·2	11·0	1931	28·1	21·1	1937	23·6	10·6
1926	23·3	12·3	1932	27·2	21·9	1938	28·0	12·8
1927	13·1	9·6	1933	26·7	19·8			

Percentage unemployed in building: Northern Ireland
1927   24·9   1933   39·3   1937   41·5

Data: Department of Employment, Northern Ireland

depression which Northern Ireland suffered during the 1920s and 1930s. It was restricted in the measures it could take by Westminster, yet it was not incapable of taking some measures had it had the will. For example, house-building came under the authority of the provincial parliament, but as the table also shows the average unemployment in the building industry in Northern Ireland was way above even the Northern Ireland general average, so that from 1921 until 1939 only 28,450 houses were built in Belfast, and of these very few were government-financed.[5] It is hardly surprising that the density of inhabitants in houses compared unfavourably with that in all other cities in the UK.[6]

It might be thought that little remained of the marginal privileges which the Protestant workers fought to maintain in the years leading to the establishment of the Northern Ireland state, yet they did remain and indeed were strengthened. The figures for housing density are a case in point, and as table 2.10 shows, the

2.10 Housing Density in Belfast: 1927, 1937

Ward	Catholic population, 1937 (per cent)	no. of rooms per person, 1926	no. of rooms per person, 1937
Falls	91	·81	·89
St Anne's	37	·88	·99
St George's	4	·84	·99
Shankill	5	·90	1·05
Smithfield	91	·72	·81
Woodvale	4	·85	·89

Data: 1926 and 1937 census, Northern Ireland

wards in Belfast which had the worst housing were also the wards with the most Catholics. Another indication of the relative conditions of the Protestant and Catholic working-class communities is provided in table 2.11, which breaks down the population in the

25

2.11   Male Population, by Age
in the Shankill and Falls Areas of
Belfast, 1937

	Falls	Shankill
0–14	5,494	4,702
15–29	3,463	4,319
30–44	2,699	3,323
45–59	1,744	2,198
60 and over	1,174	1,378
Total	14,620	15,678

Data: 1937 census, Northern Ireland

predominantly Protestant Shankill and the predominantly Catholic Falls areas, by age. The table shows that Catholics outnumbered Protestants in the non-productive, 0–14 age group, but as soon as the members of the two communities began to look for work, Protestants outnumbered Catholics.

Conditions in Northern Ireland improved after the second world war, in line with what was happening elsewhere in the world. But the relative backwardness of the Northern Ireland economy remained and so too did the relative deprivation of the Northern Ireland working class. Although male unemployment from 1946 to 1959 – 8·5 per cent on average – was lower than in the 1930s, it was still four times higher than the British average and higher than in any region in Britain. Those lucky enough to find jobs also lagged behind their British counterparts. In 1966 real income in Northern Ireland was 25 per cent below the British average,[7] a difference which remained with occasional variations for the next ten years.[8] House-building presents a similar story. In 1961 44 per cent of all dwellings in Northern Ireland had no bath and 23 per cent no inside toilet.[9] In 1969 there were still 100,000 homes – 22 per cent in all –

officially classified as unfit for habitation.[10] The lack of progress over fifty years of Unionist rule is most obviously manifest in the fact that half of all houses in Northern Ireland were over fifty years old in 1969.[11]

After 1968 the world learned to accept statements from Northern Ireland Unionists with some scepticism, but even for the Unionist government the following claim made in 1970 was breathtaking: 'The truth is that the homeless and the badly housed in Ulster have a better chance of a new house than in almost any other country in the world.'[12]

A more accurate assessment was contained in a government-commissioned report of the same year: 'The progress of slum clearing in Northern Ireland, especially in Belfast and Londonderry has been disappointingly slow.'[13]

Since 1970, when that observation was made, the position has deteriorated: in 1974 only 5,412 houses were built in the public sector compared to an average of 7,719 in the three years leading up to the report quoted above.[14]

As for the divisions within Northern Ireland, they too have remained. While the provision of the welfare state, opposed by the Unionist government at the time, lessened the pressure on working-class Catholics to leave Northern Ireland to look for jobs, a good deal of pressure remains. As table 2.12 shows, the tell-tale differences in age structure between the Catholic Falls and the Protestant Shankill still exist: the Catholic majority amongst the under-14s of 1937 has disappeared amongst the 30–59 year-olds of 1971.

The Protestant 'labour aristocracy' is still with us. Even clearer evidence is provided in table 2.13, which gives an occupational, car-ownership and community breakdown for Belfast.

The figures in tables 2.13 and 2.14 need to be qualified. The proportion of Catholics, especially in predominantly Catholic areas, is probably understated as those filling in the census were not obliged to state their religion and the 'no returns' on this question

2.12 Male Population, by Age,
in the Shankill and Falls Areas of
Belfast, 1971

	Falls	Shankill
0–14	6,341	3,578
15–19	1,802	1,302
20–29	2,599	2,207
30–44	2,282	2,739
45–49	2,021	2,698
60 and over	1,488	3,218
Total	16,513	15,742

Data: 1971 census, Northern Ireland

were much higher in the predominantly Catholic Falls than in the predominantly Protestant Shankill.

Still, a definite pattern emerges from both these tables. Apart from the small Court ward the three areas with the highest unemployment are the areas with the highest proportion of Catholics. The area with the highest proportion of managerial and self-employed (with staff) has the lowest number of Catholics. Comparing the large predominantly working-class Catholic and Protestant areas, the Falls and Shankill, Shankill has approximately double the proportion of men in foremen jobs, double the number of households with cars, half as many unemployed and twice as many owner-occupiers. The Catholics have a far lower proportion of middle-class jobs, worse housing conditions, markedly lower membership of the upper working class; Protestant privileges remain at all class levels.

Belfast is not an exception. Table 2.15 takes two small areas in County Armagh. Once more the pattern is repeated; the higher the proportion of Catholics, the more the unemployment and the worse the housing. Again in the six counties, it is the towns with large

2.13 Occupation and Religion of Men of Working Age, Belfast, 1971

	Total	Catholics	unemployed	self-employed with staff	managers	foremen supervisors	professions	households with cars
		per cent						
Clifton	15,632	34·93	9·32	2·74	3·56	3·16	0·29	43·47
Court	1,618	34·15	20·27	0·5	0·37	1·17	0·06	13·13
Cromac	6,631	27·33	7·64	2·78	5·30	2·47	4·99	48·26
Dock	2,961	62·86	17·56	0·87	1·04	1·65	0·16	14·98
Duncairn	10,396	17·37	7·29	2·73	4·04	3·57	1·56	44·26
Falls	10,138	79·02	19·64	0·86	0·94	1·67	0·17	17·44
Ormeau	12,703	14·17	5·51	2·29	3·99	3·63	1·54	46·53
Pottinger	13,392	11·64	6·98	2·49	5·16	3·60	2·23	50·75
Shankill	11,123	7·84	9·43	1·38	2·36	3·32	0·74	34·76
Smithfield	1,182	74·67	16·20	0·53	0·37	0·91	0·05	8·73
St Anne's	6,580	34·65	11·01	1·32	1·65	3·14	0·85	28·33
St George's	2,996	2·16	10·14	0·67	0·80	1·63	0·86	18·70
Victoria	10,682	3·78	5·96	2·67	5·86	3·84	3·02	53·38
Windsor	6,820	16·16	5·57	4·74	5·26	2·72	6·57	59·91
Woodvale	8,521	15·80	12·55	1·10	1·61	2·94	0·63	30·16

Data: 1971 census, Northern Ireland

2.14 Housing Conditions in Belfast, 1971

	Catholics as percentage of males of working age	no fixed bath	no hot water	no wc	inside wc	householders in shared dwellings
	per cent					
Dock	62·86	57·8	38·1	1·2	44·0	0·80
Falls	79·02	50·6	32·9	0·6	46·6	0·96
Pottinger	11·64	37·8	24·4	0·1	59·4	0·58
Shankill	7·84	48·0	28·6	0·4	51·6	0·68
Victoria	3·78	29·9	18·6	0·1	66·5	0·57

Owner-occupied houses

	total	owner-occupied
Falls	7,849	1,463
Shankill	10,633	4,095

Data: 1971 census, Northern Ireland

2.15 Socio-economic Conditions in Tandragee and Keady, County Armagh, 1971

	male population	Catholic	average persons per room	houses with no fixed bath	unemployed	households with cars
	no.		per cent			
Tandragee	1,722	283	·67	6·7	·5	77·64
Keady	2,141	1,691	·83	14·3	20·4	57·32

Data: 1971 census, Northern Ireland

Catholic majorities, Newry, Straban, Derry, which have the highest levels of unemployment. Governmental measures have done little to combat the discrepancies in unemployment. When allocating grants for new factory space, shown in table 2.16, Derry

2.16   Area of Advance Factory Space
Built by NI Government, 1945–65

	Population	Advance factory space (square feet)
Derry	53,762	455,580
Larne	16,350	777,700
Ballymena	14,734	550,000
Lurgan	17,700	541,000

Data: Sunday Times, 5 December 1971

appears to have been hard done by. Derry has a large Catholic majority; all the other towns listed have a Protestant majority. There are other differences between the two Northern Ireland communities, better publicised than the majority of tables and statistics quoted above. It is well known, for example, that under Unionism the boundaries of local government in Northern Ireland have been so drawn as to give Protestant areas a distinct advantage. In this respect the case of Derry became famous: until 1973 one third of the population had a majority on the corporation, a situation incidentally, contrived not by some bigoted Unionist of long ago but by the government of the 'liberal' Unionist, Terence O'Neill. An official British report, commissioned by the Labour government after 5 October 1968, when Catholics were a popular cause among the British intelligentsia, summarised the Northern Ireland situation conclusively:

We are satisfied that . . . the Unionist councils have used their powers to make appointments in a way which benefited Protestants. In the figures available for October 1968 only thirty per cent of Londonderry's Corporation's administrative, clerical and technical employees were Catholic. Out of the ten best paid posts only one was held by a Catholic. In Dungannon Urban District none of the council's administrative, clerical and technical employees was a Catholic. In county Fermanagh no senior posts (and relatively few others) were held by Catholics: this was rationalised by reference to 'proven loyalty' as a necessary test for local government appointments. In that county among about seventy-five drivers of school buses at most seven were Catholic. This would appear to be a very clear case of sectarian political discrimination. Armagh Urban District employed very few Catholics in salaried posts but did not appear to discriminate at lower levels. Omagh Urban District showed no clearcut pattern of discrimination though we have seen what would appear to be undoubted evidence of discrimination by Tyrone County Council.[15]

As was pointed out earlier in this chapter, discrimination at local government level did not start with the establishment of the Northern Ireland state; it was practised during the period of direct Westminster rule. What Westminster built and later permitted, the Northern Ireland Unionists merely repeated and refined.

When in 1914 the Labour Party leader Ramsay MacDonald offered the opinion that Protestants were being duped by the Tory leaders, a group of Protestant trade unionists replied: 'How can you think we hold our lives so cheap as to become the catspaws or dupes of any class or section of the community.'[16] That reply stands as well today as it did then. Of course MacDonald was right. The Protestants were being used. But that was not and is not the whole story. The Protestants have suffered a great deal from the economic and social conditions of their 'Ulster', but the fact that they have not suffered to the degree that others have has bred a politics amongst them which seeks to maintain the different levels of suffering. The Protestant worker may be called bigoted, but when he is standing in a dole queue beside a Catholic worker and it is he who gets the job and not the Catholic, to blame him for taking the job or for developing a view that he has a prior right to the job, is to ignore the size of the dole queue.

3

Leaders of the Cause

Since the 1940s the state residence of Ulster Unionism has been the government buildings at Stormont on the outskirts of Belfast. Known simply as 'Stormont', it is there that the Northern Ireland Parliament, the Assembly, and most recently the Convention, have met and deliberated. Situated at the top of a hill, at the end of a long driveway, and surrounded by green parkland, in normal times Stormont would be one of Belfast's main tourist attractions. A beautiful regal building, dubbed once as 'Ulster's White House' it looks from high over the slums and sternness of industrial Belfast; as its neighbours it has a golf course and Northern Ireland's leading public school. Above all it is a building built to last.

Stormont has been a place of pilgrimage by the Ulster faithful on many occasions during the present crisis. Demonstrations have been led to it, petitions have been handed in. While Catholics have assembled in Gaelic football grounds or walked to cemeteries, the Protestants have trekked to what they regard as 'our building', 'our parliament'.

One such demonstration occurred shortly after the Northern Ireland parliament had been suspended in March 1972. Taking place at a low point of the Ulster cause, the then leaders of the Unionist Party, right and centre, moderate and extreme, quarrelled openly with each other as to who should step on the balcony, address the multitude below and so wrest some credibility from their collective failure to maintain Stormont. For the Protestant demonstrators it was an unedifying spectacle. At one stage a group of young demonstrators wandered over to a statue of Edward Carson, and began singing, 'Come Alive, Come Alive' to the tune of the current advertising jingle for Pepsi-Cola. A neat touch there; with the fine white building reduced to a political shell, with the present leaders of the Unionist Party squabbling on the Stormont balcony, a hymn sung in exasperation to Edward Carson seemed uniquely appropriate. For the legend has it that Edward Carson, more than any other man, was responsible for the establishment of the Northern Ireland state. He was the man who had swept all before him, British prime ministers and Irish rebels included, the man who, if Ulster Protestants could countenance such 'Romanist' notions, would be their very own patron saint.

Carson is not the only such hero and like all legends the Carson one serves more to mystify than educate; but like all legends it also has some substance, for the Northern Ireland state, which Carson and his successors helped to create and sustain, reflects attitudes and an interest which were powerful in their effect.

To begin with Edward Carson is to begin at a time when Unionism in Ireland faced its greatest threat until the present. A Liberal government, dependent on the votes of the Irish nationalists, introduced in 1912 a Home Rule Bill promising Ireland limited self-government. On previous occasions similar measures had been defeated in the House of Lords, but this time, having fought an election on the issue, the Liberals had limited the Lords' veto to two years. It looked now that there was little the Unionists could do to prevent Irish self-government by 1914.

Even before the Bill was introduced the leaders of Irish Unionism had indicated that the Ulster loyalists at least would not readily accept the wishes of the British parliament, or of the Irish and British electorates. As early as September 1911, Edward Carson told a Unionist rally that if the Home Rule Bill were to become law the Unionists would ignore it and set up their own provisional government for the province of Ulster. Such threats of rebellion were repeated often in the years of crisis, 1912–21. Edward Carson even said at one stage that if the British parliament did not give the Unionists what they wanted they would have to turn to the German Kaiser. Later the same Edward Carson sat in a coalition war cabinet, waging war on the same German Kaiser. Carson's threats were not issued to amuse high Tories in Westminster tea-rooms, neither were they made to placate mass rallies of working-class Protestants. They were meant seriously, or at least Edward Carson meant them seriously. In a private letter to James Craig he wrote:

> What I am anxious about is that the people over there [Ulster] really mean to resist. I am not for a mere game of bluff and unless men are prepared to make sacrifices which they clearly understand, the talk of resistance is no use.[1]

Carson became leader of the Unionists as the Home Rule crisis was emerging. He appeared remarkably unsuitable for the position. He was not an Ulsterman; he did not sit for an Ulster constituency and although his career shows him to have had many prejudices, Protestant bigotry was not one of them. Before he adopted the Ulster cause he spent most of his time practising law in London; his constituency needed little attention as he occupied the university seat of Trinity College Dublin. Carson did not even have any particular regard for the Ulster cause, for he saw it not as an end in itself but as a tactic to be used in preventing Home Rule for the whole of Ireland, something the leaders of Unionism in Ulster were becoming less and less concerned with. But for Carson, 'If Ulster succeeds Home Rule is dead',[2] and by that he meant that successful resistance in Ulster would kill Home Rule for all of Ireland. If Carson shared nothing else with the Irish nationalists he shared a view that a divided Ireland, with one part inside the UK and one part outside was an illogicality. And indeed, when the Northern Ireland state was established and a six-county Ulster given a measure of home rule within the United Kingdom, Carson was dismissive of the scheme: 'The truth is that there is no alternative to Union unless separation and anybody who for a moment will think out the consequences will necessarily come to the same conclusion.'[3] It was not the cause of Protestant Ulster which Carson was fighting for, it was something a lot less parochial, part of the full programme of Tory reaction for which Edward Carson fought throughout his life.

In 1892, when Carson first entered parliament as a Liberal Unionist he represented a number of landlords on the Evicted Tenants' Commission, a body established by the Liberal government to consider the claims of the Irish tenants. Among his clients was Lord Clanricord, described once as 'the best hated landlord of his time'.[4] The following year Carson combined a defence of press baronage with an attack on the trade unions when he appeared for the *Evening News*, then being sued by the trade unionist and Liberal MP, Havelock Wilson. He helped to defend Jameson of the Jameson Raid, one of the most blatant examples of British imperialist aggression. He was also a leading spokesman for repressive Victorian morality when he led the prosecution in the Oscar Wilde homosexuality trials.

Such a record did not go unnoticed and Carson was appointed Solicitor General in the Tory government of 1900. This second career, his parliamentary one, provides a further testament for reaction. In 1894 he voted against the reduction of miners' hours. Two years later he voted against a Tory Land Bill because, he said, it was injurious to the interests of the landlords. In 1900 he led the Tory attack on the Trades Disputes Act which sought to restore to trade unions the right to picket without being sued, and in 1908 he voted against the introduction of old age pensions. But attacking trade unionists, pensioners and tenants were not the only causes which Toryism was promoting. The Anglican church, an important part of the English establishment, was defended by Carson in 1893 when he voted against both Scottish and Welsh disestablishment. Finally, he opposed any move to democratise parliament: in 1893 and 1906 he opposed the proposal that MPs should be paid a salary; in 1894 he supported postponement of electoral reform; and in 1908 and 1913 he voted against the abolition of plural voting. His philosophy is best expressed in his own words. In 1912 when Poor Law reform was under debate Carson advocated: 'The able bodied paupers if well conducted might be placed in labour colonies, if ill-conducted in detention centres.'[5] And in 1933 at the annual Tory conference, when advocating an iron hand in India, he proclaimed support for 'Our friends first, our friends second and our friends third'.[6]

There was then, no contradiction in Carson being prepared to enlist the Kaiser in his support one year, and wage war against him the next. The interest in each case was the same. On the one hand the interests of the British upper class against those of the German upper class; on the other the British and Irish upper class against the majority of the Irish people. No contradiction, no paradox. The principle – perpetuation of the British establishment's rule – was the same.

This is why, once partition was agreed and a majority of the counties of Ireland won a kind of independence, Carson was no longer interested in the cause of Ulster. For him, the greater battle, preventing Home Rule for the whole of Ireland, had been lost. So he left Northern Ireland to be lorded over by others, in particular to James Craig, its first Prime Minister.

Like Carson, Craig (later Lord Craigavon) occupies a sanctified place in the Ulster Protestant's hall of fame; to the extent that in the hey-day of Terence O'Neill's 'liberalism', when everybody was urged to forget past prejudices and work together for the new Ulster, the first new town in Northern Ireland was named 'Craigavon'. Craig shared with Carson the leadership of the Ulster rebellion. Craig was the organiser, Carson the charismatic leader. But there the similarity between the two ends. While Carson represented the Anglo-Irish and high Tory establishment, James Craig's interests were firmly embedded in Ulster itself. A millionaire industrialist, he used Unionism to defend the economic and political supremacy of Belfast's industrial bourgeoisie, and since that needed the support of the Protestant working class, and needed it despite the wretched economic and social conditions of that working class, 'fenian-bashing' came to play the organising role. The mechanics of that policy will be dealt with later, but it is only fair to the memory of Lord Craigavon that his particular contribution to the tactics of divide and rule should be briefly recorded, a contribution of a particular malevolent and vicious variety.

The viciousness can be illustrated by Craig's words and actions during the major outbreak of sectarian warfare in Belfast in the years 1920–22. It occurred while the War of Independence was being waged in the south, but unlike what was happening in the rest of Ireland the Belfast 'troubles' were of a specifically sectarian nature. They were sparked off at a meeting of a group of shipyard workers in July 1920 which demanded that all Catholic workers leave the yards. As Protestant workers tried to enforce the demand a Catholic worker shouted 'up the rebels'. Two years of anti-Catholic violence followed. Craig encouraged it in two ways; first he publicly approved the actions of the Protestant shipyard workers;[7] second he promoted the idea of a special constabulary to deal with Catholic opponents to Unionism – a part of which was to become the infamous 'B Specials' and which formed an exclusively Protestant paramilitary wing of the Northern Ireland state until it was disbanded by the British Labour government during 1969–70.

Although it was during Craig's premiership, 1921–40, that the Northern Ireland state institutionalised not only the violence against Catholics, but all the other means of discrimination, and although Craig's rhetoric was repeatedly and publicly anti-nationalist and pro-British, he often expressed different attitudes. In private conversation with the southern Irish civil servant, G.C. Duggan, he opined, 'Duggan, you know that in this island we cannot always be separate from each other. We are too small to be apart.'[8] On another occasion, when there was a wrangle over the amount of money the Northern Ireland government should receive from Westminster, Craig warned:

> Ulster having emerged from the many other difficulties which surrounded her and having vindicated her determination to remain part of Great Britain and the Empire, might find herself so financially hampered that she could not carry on as a definite subordinate unit.[9]

His Unionism was neither unconditional nor definitive. For Craig and the people he represented, Ulster Unionism was no more an end in itself than it was for Edward Carson.

But as with Carson, James Craig's portrait remains standing and revered on the sideboards of Protestant Ulster. It is there because whatever the intricacies of his political creed he was seen by the Protestant working class to be a leader who put the Catholics in their place, and kept them there; someone who was not afraid to gloat: 'I have always said that I am an Orangeman first and a politician afterwards, all I boast is that we are a Protestant Parliament for a Protestant state.'[10]

Such sentiments are the stuff from which Protestant folk heroes are made and Craig was by no means alone in voicing them. Basil Brooke, later Lord Brookeborough, who three years after Craig's death became Northern Ireland's third Prime Minister (the second was the 70-year-old and deaf John Andrews) had made his reputation in the 1930s when he advocated a policy of selective employment to stem Protestant working-class disaffection from the Unionist Party:

> Many in the audience employ Catholics, but I have not one about the house. . . . In Northern Ireland the Catholic population is increasing to a great extent. Ninety-seven per cent of Roman Catholics in Ireland are disloyal and disruptive. . . . If we in Ulster allow Roman Catholics to work on our farms we are traitors to Ulster.[11]

What Brooke preached he also practised, and although his twenty years of premiership introduced little that was new into Northern Ireland Unionism, discrimination against Catholics in jobs, housing and voting rights was consolidated. This was sufficient for Brooke's name to be added to the litany of exemplary leaders intoned by the loyalist pilgrims of the late 1960s and early 1970s when praying for the second coming of 'traditional Unionism'.

None prayed louder, both for traditional Unionism and for

many other traditions than the Reverend Doctor, Ian Kyle Paisley, who, as the crisis of Ulster Unionism developed and Protestant Ulster felt badly in need of heroes offered himself for the role. No one has shouted louder and longer than Ian Paisley about the 'betrayals of the "liberals" ' – O'Neill, Chichester-Clark and Brian Faulkner – and although Paisley's following can be attributed to many factors one of the more prominent is that he was warning the Unionist party about the direction Terence O'Neill was leading it years before the streets of Belfast echoed to the shouts of 'O'Neill Must Go'. As early as 1964 Paisley led protests against the display of the Irish tricolour in the election headquarters of the Republican Party. When O'Neill, under pressure from the British government, agreed to certain minimal reforms and was seen to be compromising with the Catholic opposition rather than repressing it as Craig and Brooke had done, Ian Paisley became the prophet fulfilled. His stature and his following grew enormously as the crisis developed. By placing himself firmly in the tradition of Carson, Craig and Brooke, the 'Big Man' became the standard-bearer for Unionism, and when that became a dirty word, a standard-bearer for the loyalists.

But whatever Ian Paisley may be he is no Carson, Craig or Brooke. Past leaders of the Unionist cause all represented the rulers: Carson was a high Tory, Craig and Andrews the industrialists, Brooke the landed lord. Each could have found himself on the Tory front bench at Westminster – as indeed Carson did. Ian Paisley is not cast in that mould. He is no establishment figure. In the past he has been eager to take on anybody he judges to be backsliding, from the Archbishop of Canterbury to the Duke of Edinburgh, whom Paisley once accused of having 'a streak of republicanism'.[12] And while Carson, Craig and Brooke were products and guardians of an economic and social order that has parallels in many places, Ian Paisley is a peculiarly Ulster phenomenon, who sees himself as leading a peculiarly Ulster crusade. As he explained in one of the earliest editions of his newspaper, the *Protestant Telegraph*:

We pledge ourselves to expose the forces of evil men and leaders who are the enemies of Ulster and true Protestantism. We will not shun the biblical command to be faithful and we will seek by God's help to reveal the hidden things of darkness, so that in the power of God the strongholds of Satan may be pulled down and a faithful testimony of God raised in our land.[13]

All of this may seem a long way from standing in a parliamentary election against Terence O'Neill, but Ian Paisley was not only standing against someone with whom he had political differences, he was standing against someone whom he judged to be 'a coward and a puppet of the Pope'.[14] Similarly when Paisley thundered against the Catholic church he was not criticising a religious institution or an erroneous interpretation of the bible, he was taking on the Devil himself: 'Through Popery the Devil has shut up the way to our inheritance. Priestcraft, superstition and papalism with all their attendant voices of murder, theft, immorality, lust and incest, blocked the way to the land of gospel liberty.'[15] For Ian Paisley the land of gospel liberty was the six counties of Ulster – a land of good living, high church attendence, where religion and state were an indissoluble entity. Long before the Civil Rights movement, long before the surrenders of Terence O'Neill, Paisley had established himself as the guardian of that entity and anyone who came to Ulster preaching a different doctrine had to engage the self-styled Moderator of the Free Presbyterian Church. In 1959 when the liberal Protestant minister Donald Soper visited the Ulster bible-belt town of Ballymena, it was Ian Paisley who threw a bible at him for daring to question the literal truth of the Good Book. In 1967 when the leading ecumenist, Dr John Moorman, Bishop of Ripon, announced that he intended to visit Ulster, it was Ian Paisley's threats and warnings that caused him to cancel the visit. It was not only 'Romanising' Protestants or compromising politicians that the Reverend Doctor included in his list of adversaries. The conspiracy against Protestant Ulster was much more serious than that:

Nearly all the methods of propaganda are now firmly controlled by the Roman Catholic Church – cinema, television, newspapers and magazines. Their representatives were carefully selected while posts were being prepared in political parties, trade unions, universities and Protestant churches. Northern Ireland, being the last bulwark of Protestantism in Europe, if not the world, was singled out for special attention.[16]

Basing himself on this theory, almost everything that happened both inside and outside Ireland is seen by Paisley as a Roman plot, from the murder of John Kennedy[17] to the Vietnam War, which 'must be seen as an attempt by the Vatican to exercise her political power.'[18] But to be fair it was not a purely Roman plot; others were involved:

> Watch the Jews . . . Israel is on the way back to favour. . . . Watch the Papist Rome rising to a grand crescendo with the Communists. The Reds are on the march. They are heading for an alliance against the return of the Lord Jesus Christ.[19]

How the Catholic Church, communism and Israel are compatible, Dr Paisley has yet to make clear, but the relationship between Catholicism and Marxism was elaborated in one of the *Protestant Telegraph*'s more memorable passages:

> Both Romanism and Communism have absorbed the basic elements of pagan philosophy to bolster up their false and anti-God systems. Rome deployed and developed Pagan ritual within the framework of counterfeit Christianity. Communism, prior to the French revolution adopted the pagan and pantheistic doctrine of creation. The resulting formula came to be known as dialectical materialism.[20]

Paisley saw himself ordained to fight this dreadful conspiracy. For him traditional Unionism had 'a sanctified and religious identity'.[21] His own particular brand had a special grace: 'it was only by the providence of almighty God that the *Protestant Telegraph* was not stillborn'.[22] As for the paper itself it poured out article after article with such headings as, 'The Love Affairs of the Vatican',[23] 'Priestly

Murders Exposed'[24] and 'Children Tortured – Monks Turned Out as Sadists'.[25]

All of which may appear slightly sick and certainly comical, to anyone not born and bred in Northern Ireland. But Ian Paisley is no figure of fun; the paranoid Calvinist side of his character gave him a solid base among the God-fearing, Devil-hating sections of the Protestant working class and petty-bourgeoisie.

In the 1960s these people had seen their safe, narrow world begin to crumble. Their religious leaders had started talking with the dreaded Catholic church. A new morality was challenging the puritan ethic passed on from parents to children. On top of all that came the political policies of Terence O'Neill – talking with Sean Lemass, Prime Minister of the Catholic Irish Republic, visiting convents. The Ulster Protestant could close his or her eyes to the new permissiveness of 'Swinging Britain'; could even ignore the betrayals of the Protestant Church leaders in England, because although such cancers touched Ulster, they did not heavily affect it. But Terence O'Neill with his policies of conciliation and, later, Brian Faulkner with his power-sharing – they were impossible to ignore. The cancer was spreading and was threatening the very existence of Northern Ireland, 'the last bulwark of Protestantism in Europe, if not in the world'.

Ian Paisley spoke out and acted against all that. Protestant evangelists do not make up the majority of Protestants in Northern Ireland and it is not the defence of the social morality and the Protestant ethic which motivates the majority of working-class Protestants, but there are enough evangelists and enough moral outrage to have given Ian Paisley a hearing and a following, and when he turned his brilliant oratory, his destructive wit and his political attention to the Unionist traitors, many more listened and followed. What the 'Big Man' promised was salvation; salvation from heretical faiths, and from political compromisers:

> And there was wee Brian Faulkner, sitting on a great big chair, looking just as proud as the Pope of Rome himself – and his wee

44

legs were wrapped round the legs of the chair, and I said to my companion, either we're going to have to saw his legs off, or the chair's legs off, to get him off that chair.[26]

Paisley was not the only person who threw Brian Faulkner off his chair. The final straw which broke Faulkner's back, the Ulster Workers' Council strike, was initially not supported by Paisley. But he was quick to jump on the bandwagon once the strike began to spread. This is just one example of how politically adept Paisley has become in the last seven years. So much so that the man who always appeared on television wearing a dog-collar, and passed through a stage of wearing a dog-collar some of the time, now wears a collar and tie all the time.

What has aided Paisley in this metamorphosis from religious nutcase to political animal is his intimate knowledge of his audience – the Protestant petty-bourgeoisie and working class. Unlike Craig or Brooke, Ian Paisley has not relied on a simple diet of 'fenian-bashing' to sustain him. He has an excellent record as a constituency MP, he is a constant questioner of the government on housing and other facilities. He has even campaigned for the nationalisation of Lough Neagh fishing grounds. When he formed the Democratic Unionist Party he went on record as wanting no links with the Orange Order, saying its link with the Unionist Party was undemocratic. Even more surprising is his consistent opposition to internment, an opinion which few Protestants shared when it was first introduced, but which many came to share when Protestants started to be interned. So Paisley cannot be dismissed as a selfseeking populist; indeed in 1971 he surprised many people by adopting a conciliatory tone towards the Irish Republic:

If the 1937 Constitution of the Republic was scrapped and if it came to be seen that the Catholic hierarchy no longer exercised the power, influence and control over the government of Dublin then Protestants in Northern Ireland would look upon the Republic in a different light and there would be good neighbour-liness in the highest possible sense.[27]

That one sentence produced whoops of delight amongst Irish nationalists at the time, who rushed to the conclusion that the Protestant demagogue was softening on the issue of a united Ireland. Their expectations were to be dashed the following week when a bold front page headline in the *Protestant Telegraph* proclaimed, 'No To a United Ireland'.[28]

Having approached the abyss the Reverend Doctor hastily retreated from it, for, while he is prepared at times to take risks, he is careful never to run ahead of his constituency.

It is not easy to fit a label on to Paisley. He has been dubbed a fascist and evidence for this can be adduced from his support for Ian Smith and for the South African regime; yet the explanation of that support does not lie in his approval of racialism and dictatorship, rather in the fact that the ruling classes of those regimes share the same Calvinistic religion of Paisley. In the final analysis it is within that Calvinism that the key to an understanding of Ian Paisley lies. He sees himself above all as the preacher, the shepherd. His flock is surrounded by mortal enemies, but Ian Paisley will lead it to safety. Not for him the suicide pact of an independent Ulster, but rather the security of a Northern Ireland fully integrated into the United Kingdom.

Paisley has not been shy of leading his flock through blood. As early as 1966, one of the members of a UVF gang which murdered a Catholic barman declared that he wished he had never heard of Ian Paisley. In November 1969 Ian Paisley personally led a gang of thugs, armed with sticks, into the centre of Armagh in an attempt to prevent a Civil Rights march from entering the city. Then, in January 1972, it was Ian Paisley who announced that if the army would not deal with an anti-internment march to be held in Derry, he would; the army, by fourteen deaths to nil, dealt with it.

Such is the other side of Ian Paisley, and such too is the further side of the people he leads and represents. He is not just one of the leaders of the Protestant lower classes, he is a product and manifestation of a large section of them. Unlike Edward Carson, James Craig or Basil Brooke, Paisley is of the people in whose name he speaks, which is one reason he will be there at the end, whenever that is. He is the lower-class Ulster Protestant. He shares with them an occasional potential for progressiveness, but is, like them, overburdened with sectarianism, violence and selfrighteousness. If Edward Carson can serve as an introduction to British imperialism, and James Craig as an introduction to Ulster capitalism, Ian Paisley is the best introduction to what the consciousness of large sections of the Protestant poor is all about.

4

The Protestant Way of Life

1969 to 1974 were bad years for the Protestants of Northern Ireland. Their parliament was suspended, their B Specials were disbanded, their city corporation in Derry was dissolved, their political leaders compromised, even an occasional Orange march was banned. And, on top of all that, Linfield Football Club managed to win the (Northern) Irish League only once.

To those not well acquainted with Northern Ireland society, lack of a football team's success may appear of little consequence compared to the headline-capturing political developments. But for many working-class Protestants in Belfast, Linfield's failures were as big a blow to self-esteem as was the breakup of their political system. Football, like most other things in Northern Ireland, is partitioned, with a political and religious symbolism of its own. Catholics are not supposed to engage in such 'foreign' games as soccer, though most ignore that stricture; but since 1949 when the 'Catholic' football team, Belfast Celtic, withdrew from the Irish League after their players had been attacked by Linfield fans, Catholics in Belfast have not had a readily identifiable team to cheer. But for Protestants, *the* team is Linfield, the equivalent of Glasgow Rangers in Scotland, and like them adorned in shirts of royal blue, white shorts and red socks. All the old Protestant songs are heard at Linfield matches, mingled with chants copied from the English teams and their fans as seen on television. In addition Linfield fans have their own specialities, such as:

> There are no Fenians in our team,
> In our team, in our team,
> There are no Fenians in our team,
> No! No! No![1]

Although this is not quite the case and Linfield, unlike Rangers, have never had a policy of not employing Catholics, it is an academic point for the Linfield fans, the Protestant working-class youths of west Belfast who carry huge Union Jacks and wear blue scarves tinged with red and white as a badge of distinction. In the past the fans have had every reason to wear their team's colours with pride, because Linfield were the giants of Northern Ireland football, winning the Irish League 28 times before the 1969–70 season. A microcosm of the Protestant cause in Northern Ireland, Linfield reigned supreme and appeared unchallengeable.

Midway through the 1960s things started to go wrong. A football analyst could explain the decline in his language: the ageing of the team, managerial problems, etc., but for the fans the decline of Linfield was one more affront, one more assault from the forces of darkness. Despite the setbacks on the football field the fans still marched like some victorious army from Linfield's home ground in south-west Belfast to the Shankill Road, the capital of Protestant Ulster after every home game. The parade has led to more than one riot in recent years, yet it has now become as traditional as the Orange marches themselves, and no 'true Blue' Linfield fan would think of travelling the mile and a half to the Shankill any other way. One report of such a procession in 1971 described how the fans would chant:

> Who are we? Linfield, Linfield.
> What are we ? Champions! Champions!

The report went on to note that at the time Linfield were neither champions of the Irish League nor the current League leaders, but then the chant was not confined to the fortunes of the football team. The slogan was an assertion by the Protestants of the Shankill, alluding as much to themselves as to Linfield Football Club; they were 'Champions! Champions!'

That is what the Protestant culture is all about: Protestant supremacy, Protestant ascendency. The Linfield team is merely a part of that ascendency. The belief in it protrudes into every aspect of contemporary Protestant working-class life: the team, the songs, the humour. The over-riding message is the excellence of the Protestants. As a recent loyalist song puts it:

> Proud and defiant,
> With folk self-reliant,
> A Loyalist giant,
> That's Ulster.[2]

Nor is this self-image confined to the working class balladeers of Belfast. Terence O'Neill, now regarded as a Protestant heretic, expressed the loyalist view well:

> It is frightfully hard to explain to Protestants that if they give Roman Catholics a good house they will live like Protestants, because they will see neighbours with cars and television sets. They will refuse to have eighteen children, but if a Roman Catholic is jobless and lives in the most ghastly hovel he will rear eighteen children on National Assistance. If you treat Roman Catholics with due consideration they will live like Protestants in spite of the authoritarian nature of their Church.[3]

There are countless other examples of this view in the loyalist newspapers which have sprung up in the last few years: the Protestants are clean, tidy, 'self-reliant'; the Catholics are dirty, undisciplined and live off National Assistance. In one of the most popular of the Protestant newspapers a typical member of the IRA is depicted in this fashion:

Rank status of the I Ran Away Army: final week.
Type: Gunman.
Rank: El Supremo.
Qualifications: Non-worker, large family, can quote buro* rules backwards, under 5ft 2in.
Uniform: Felt hat, dirty raincoat, running shoes.
Habits: Washes once a year, whether dirty or not.

* Buro – employment exchange.

Points of Recognition: Two yellow streaks down back, kicks cats and old ladies when really angry.

How to Destroy: Shout UVF at him but don't approach for he will have a brown operation! ! !

You will have noticed that all the IRA are small men, this lends itself to the rebel anthem, Soldiers are Wee.[4]

Loyalist newspapers return to the washing habits of Catholics time and time again. In one joke an IRA man is pictured talking to another:

> Here is a letter to Strasbourg telling how the British torture us every morning.
> Torture us? How?
> They make us wash don't they?[6]

Being dirty and smelly is by no means all of it. While many Belfast Protestants are no mean drinkers themselves, the Catholic, especially the Catholic politician, is always pictured as an alcoholic:

> John Hume's confessional: Don't pay any attention to what I promise, father, about going teetotal – it's only the drink talking.[6]

And naturally on top of all this the Catholics are stupid. Racist jokes about the Irish which circulate in England are retold by Protestants with the proviso that the Irish in question are Catholic:

> A Belfast Republican docker was walking along the Quay kicking a tortoise. A policeman watched for a few minutes and then went up to the rebel and asked: 'Why are you kicking that poor defenceless tortoise?' Rebel: 'It's been following me around all day'.[7]

Songs take up the same refrain. One, 'The Battle of the Diamond', speaks of 'craven papists' and 'papist fools'; another, 'The Eighth of December', mentions 'papish knaves'; another, 'The Origins of Orangeism', tells of 'traitors vile'. These are traditional Orange ballads that have been sung for years. More recent collections carry on the tradition. A song-book published by the Ulster Defence Association in 1974 refers to 'filthy rebel scum' and 'dirty fenian swine'.[8] If Catholics are inferior, vermin and swine they should be treated accordingly. A song celebrating the burning down of Catholic houses in Bombay Street, Belfast in 1969 includes:

> On the 14th August we took a little trip,
> Up along Bombay Street and burned out all
>   the shit,
> We took a little petrol and we took a little gun,
> And we fought the bloody fenians, till we had
>   them on the run.[9]

There is no question of treating the Catholics like human beings, or even like an enemy and offering them a fair fight, because:

> I was born under the Union Jack
> I was born under the Union Jack,
> If Taigs are made for killing,
> The blood is made to flow,
> You've never seen a place like Sandy Row.

> I was born under the Union Jack,
> I was born under the Union Jack,
> If guns are made for shooting,
> Then skulls are made to crack.
> You've never seen a better Taig,
> Than with a bullet in his back.[10]

Shooting people in the back is hardly the sort of activity one boasts about, unless, of course the victims are inferior beings. But if they are, all manner of extermination is justified:

> We killed 10,000 fenians,
> Their flag of truce was raised,
> So now 10,000 fenians,
> Are lying in the grave.[11]

So the Catholics are drunken, filthy, cowardly fenian scum

who should be put down by any and all available means. By contrast, Protestants appear a superior species, superior not only in washing and behaviour, but in every other aspect: 'If there are 13 cows in a field you can easily recognise the Ulster Loyalist bull — He'll be the one that is still standing'.[12] Superior potency is an essential ingredient of any self-constructed master race, as is superior restraint. So, for the Protestants of Northern Ireland, it is the Catholics who are licentious. In 1972 when the British press was building up the middle-class housewives' 'Women Together' movement as something that would shame the IRA into peace, a loyalist newspaper carried a joke about a woman in the Catholic working-class district of Andersonstown grabbing a representative of Women Together and saying, 'Listen ducky, if we get peace our men will be released and I'll have to give up my 14 Welsh regiment boyfriends.'[13]

As for Protestant women, well they are the sweet-tempered, faithful lassies of the Protestant male dream. The following song shows how differently the Protestant culture presents 'rebel' and loyalist women and how the Ulster Protestant sees the role of women generally in the loyalist order of things. (The 'Prentice' of the song is shorthand for the Apprentice Boys, a Protestant institution similar to the Orange Order.)

The 'Prentice Girls

It cheers an honest 'Prentice Boy,
Above all other joys,
To act an independent part,
With comrade 'Prentice Boys.
But O! we prize that sister link,
Of lovely living pearls,
Right joyously we rise and drink,
To Derry's 'Prentice Girls.

Though thoughtless flirts and dainty dames,
Of Irish birth and blood,

Look coldly on the hopes and aims,
Of our dear sisterhood,
We'll have their sympathy to cheer
Their sweethearts through all perils,
To us you're doubly near and dear,
Old Derry's 'Prentice girls.

Their mothers proved, long, long ago,
Fit mates for gallant men,
And if their daughters are but tried,
They'll prove as true again.
Through every struggle for our cause,
Since famous eighty-eight,
We've had fair women's sweet applause
Our hearts to stimulate.[14]

There are occasions when this picture of servitude and tranquillity are rudely interrupted. The narrative in a recent loyalist song, 'It's All Over', tells of such an occurrence. The singer, a Protestant internee who learns that his wife has been unfaithful, begins the last verse with the usual maudlin self-pity familiar in all such songs wherever they are written:

I didn't think my wife would be unfaithful,
I always thought that she would play the game.

He then changes abruptly in the final two lines, when the masterly male vows to take revenge on his property:

But when they let me out of Long Kesh prison,
I'll make her wish she'd never heard my name.[15]

In song at least, the Protestant male reigns supreme; he deals out rough justice to the inferior Catholic; Catholic women are 'flighty' and whores; and while the Protestant women are usually virtuous and adoring they too will be quickly put in their place should any of them step out of line. But this is not only in song. One amusing example of the way the Protestant values affect behaviour occurred in the early 1960s when Ian Paisley was considering standing for the Belfast Corporation, but instead allowed his wife to stand. The result would still indicate Paisley's popularity but a defeat for his wife would not be as ego-shattering as one for her mighty husband. Other sections of Protestant male society allow their faithful women-folk even less scope. While women members of the IRA can be in 'active service units' as the euphemism goes, the UDA claim that their women's section is exclusively confined to 'welfare work and first aid'.[16] Not that this is always strictly the case, as was shown in 1974 when UDA women tortured and murdered Anne Ogilby as a punishment for supposedly carrying on an affair with a married Protestant internee. Even then the twisted logic remained untouched: it was fair game for UDA women to punish their own for stepping outside the male morality; it would not infringe upon the monopoly of violence permitted to the men of the UDA.

Women are allotted a similar role in the Orange Order. They are not allowed to take part in any of the Orange demonstrations and the functions of the Ladies Orange Association are, in the words of the present Grand Secretary of the Orange Order, 'fund raising, they are very generous to charities.'[17]

The Orange Order illustrates much more of the Protestant way of life than simply the position in it of women. The Order's clearest area of influence is political, manifested in its right to 122 delegates, or 10 to 20 per cent of all delegates (depending on the attendance) at meetings of the Ulster Unionist Council, theoretically the governing body of the Unionist Party. However incongruous it might seem that a supposedly religious organisation should exercise authority in a governing political party in twentieth-century western Europe, there is no doubt that the Orange Order has earned that right, for it has served the cause of the Unionist establishment long and well. Its very foundation in the late eighteenth century was a counter-revolutionary response to the activities of the United Irishmen. A hundred years later it was to the forefront in opposing the Ballot Act, arguing that the secret ballot would, 'hand over the representation of Ireland to the priests'. As a leading Orangeman declared, in reply to the argument that in public voting landlords influenced the way their tenants voted, 'Votes were given to a minority to be exercised for the benefit of the majority, and should therefore be in public and not in secret. I believe landlords have a legitimate influence.'[18] The Order's sympathies with the cause of Irish landlordism were even more manifest during the 1880s when an Orange leader, the Reverend R. Kane, suggested that a priest be killed for every landlord killed during the 'Land War' (see chapter 8). Although the Order did not take up this advice officially, it did organise the transportation of scab labourers to farms which had been boycotted in the south and west of Ireland. In the middle of that decade the Orange Order healed the then prevailing three-way split in Unionism between the Tories, the Liberal Unionists and the Order itself. Later, in the early years of this century, the Orange organisation was used to recruit Protestants to the armed wing of Unionism, the Ulster Volunteer Force (see chapter 7); and during the establishment of the Northern Ireland state its para-military wing, the Ulster Special Constabulary, was recruited in Orange halls. In 1933 the Order was prominent in smashing the temporary unity of the Belfast working class which led to joint Protestant–Catholic rioting over unemployment (see chapter 7).

Although such a record explains the Order's special influence in the political structure of Northern Ireland, it does not convey in full the attraction it exercises on less privileged sections of the Protestant community. Naturally some of that attraction lies in the Order's very special relationship with the governing circles of Unionism, since in the circumstances membership creates the illusion of being part of the ruling circle, part of the state machine. And it is not entirely an illusion. Until very recently membership of the Orange Order was obligatory for political advancement. It also helped in the more mundane matters: in getting employment, in receiving council houses. In all, the Orange Order was an integral part of the state machine and membership of it meant a claim on that state machine.

There are other reasons for its attraction. The Orange Lodges provide a social life, a meeting-place, a club, where the Protestant worker can feel he is something special – the white man's club where none of Ulster's niggers darken the door. The Order adds a dash of colour to the otherwise drab life of the ordinary working man. The drums, the coloured sashes, the marches.

The marches sum it all up. There are over 1,500 Orange Lodges in Northern Ireland, all of them heavily engaged in arranging the profusion of Orange demonstrations during the spring and summer. The Lodges are not conspiratorial meeting-places whose members formally discuss the best way of putting down the fenians. It is not like that at all. The typical Lodge meeting opens with a hymn and a prayer, followed by the initiation of new members, who are given a standard address on the principles of Orangeism. The rest of the meeting is taken up with various details of administration, and in particular the planning of the marches. No 'political' motions are debated at Lodge meetings. Indeed it all seems very mundane, which is why meetings are usually poorly attended. The political power which the Orange Order exercises is not to be found at the level of the local Lodge but much further up the Order's hierarchical ladder. What the average Lodge member is given is marches.

On 12 July 1975 an estimated 100,000 people took part in the various Orange marches. In the past these demonstrations have been invariably addressed by Northern Ireland's Prime Minister – an opportunity for him to renew his contract with the Protestant faithful. They march in their best suits, many wearing bowler hats, symbol of a more privileged people. Some carry swords; they all have their sashes, and march behind beautifully woven banners adorned with the images of the kings and queens of England, open bibles and obscure religious gentlemen of long ago. Each Lodge is preceded by a band thumping out the ascendency songs. The drum is the dominant instrument; and although none of the songs is actually sung on the marches, the message comes through clearly in the tunes which are played: 'Croppies Lie Down', 'No Surrender'. The marches are well ordered, disciplined, almost military; at the same time the long procession exudes a carnival atmosphere. It is a rally of the victorious. The marchers may attend their Lodge meetings rarely but on the 'Twelfth' they don sash and demonstrate. For such is their birthright. A hundred thousand people may march but it is the exclusiveness which appeals. You cannot buy or bribe your way into the Orange Order, you are born into it, like into a white skin. The fact that the material benefits from Orangeism are marginal means nothing to the ordinary Protestant worker on the Twelfth. Like the Linfield fan he tastes power, glory, supremacy:

> Stout hearted in battle and stout handed too,
> The Protestant boys are true to the last.
> And faithful and peaceful when danger has passed,
> And oh, they bear,
> And proudly wear,
> The colours that floated o'er many a fray,
> When cannons were flashing,
> And sabres were clashing,
> The Protestant boys still carried the day.[19]

Formally the Orange Order's aims are religious: nothing less than the defence of the Reformation. But even the Order does not cover the roles that religion plays in the life of the ordinary Protestant, for its manifestations are everywhere. Ian Paisley's church on the Ravenhill Road in Belfast cost £175,000 to build, which makes it the most expensive piece of religious architecture to be built in the British Isles since the second world war, except for the Catholic cathedral in Liverpool and the Anglican cathedral in Coventry. A survey carried out between December 1968 and January 1969 by the Opinion Research Centre found that 75 per cent of those questions considered themselves 'very or fairly religious' compared with 58 per cent in Britain. Only 25 per cent of the British sample believed that the miracles in the Bible really happened, but in Northern Ireland 68 per cent were convinced that the miracles were literally true.[20] All the Loyalist newspapers of recent years have what amounts to a 'Church Correspondent', and any random selection will show what this means. In an organ of the Ulster Volunteer Force (Mk II), one of the most sectarian of the groups, there is half a page on the meaning of a psalm alongside the usual anti-rebel articles;[21] and in an issue of the Woodvale Defence Association's newspaper the following advice is offered:

> It was good to see that the Grand [Orange] Lodge has rejected the Westminster White Paper; what a pity it did not go one step further and also reject the use of the Ecumenical Common Bible which is being used in place of the Authorised Version in many of the Orange Lodges today. This common ecumenical bible is a blatant encroachment upon the glorious Protestant faith.[22]

The most popular word in the vocabulary of the 'good Protestant' is 'saved': from the hoardings of the small mission halls to those at the large churches, the posters ring out, 'HAVE YOU BEEN SAVED?'. Saved, that is, from hell and damnation. It is a religion of fear; over-riding fear of the unknown, a religion that stresses the need to be ever on guard against assaults from the powers of darkness. Of course the Devil masterminds the anti-God aggression but, for a religion of dread to be sustaining, a more immediate, more visible ogre is needed. In Protestant Northern Ireland this ogre is the Pope of Rome himself, not just a bad theologian, not just the titular head of a large church, but the anti-Christ of the biblical prophecies. With such a real and dreadful enemy, which, moreover, the rest of the world tolerates or even applauds, 'salvation' is all the more urgent. For the Calvinist the way to such salvation is obvious and simple: accept Jesus Christ as your saviour, read the bible and believe all that is written. Not only will you be rewarded in the after-life, you will receive material benefits on earth, for God is on your side:

> Against the Turks, Jews and Infidels,
> We always have to fight,

To let the wondering world know,
We're always in the right.
Search the scriptures over,
It is there to be found,
That the tree that bears no fruit,
It ought to be cut down.[23]

Naturally Ulster has a special place in God's scheme of things. The following two lines come not from a religious tract but from the newspaper of the Vanguard Party (former leader, William Craig), one of the most important political organisations in Northern Ireland:

Open our eyes to His light above,
Shone always on Ulster by his angels of love.[24]

And within Ulster the Protestant is on a higher religious, moral and intellectual plane than anyone else:

We want no Popish tyrant priest
To guide us on our way;
We know not how to count the beads,
Such trash we throw away;
To idols dumb and gods of stone,
We'll never bend the knee,
Nor say confessions in the dark;
Our consciences are free.[25]

Obviously not all Protestants in Northern Ireland sport the religious self-righteousness of the songs and poems quoted above, but many do, and many of the others share the exclusiveness of those who do, who are proud to boast that they are 'saved'. It is an exclusiveness that fires the Linfield fans, that cements the values of the Orangemen, that sustains the male dominance of the Protestant warriors. It is not confined to the social and religious structures. It has many parallels in the educational structure which dictates that Catholics go to one set of schools and Protestants to another.

It would be wrong to lay the blame for segregated schooling solely or even primarily at the door of the Orange bosses. The Catholic church has been as responsible for it as any other group or institution. Its hierarchy was always resisted and continues to resist any scheme which may lessen their control over 'their' people or put at risk the supposedly fragile souls of the Catholic Irish. However, the Unionist government has appeared quite happy to go along with them, has given generous grants to the Catholic schools, and in return sanctioned the propagandising of the Protestant view of things in the state system. Perhaps the best example is the manner in which history is taught in the state schools. Irish history scarcely appears on the syllabus, except at the highest age levels and in relation to English history. The series of standard text books used at the lower age levels is entitled 'Britain's Heritage'. It offers the usual eulogy of British heroes, but little else. The first book in the series, dealing with the years 2,500 BC to AD 1453, has chapters entitled 'England and Wales' and 'England and Scotland'. There is no chapter on England and Ireland. Similarly the volume which deals with the eighteenth century has a chapter on Clive's conquest of India but makes no mention of Ireland under the repressive Penal Laws. In the last few years, Irish history has entered the syllabus of the Northern Ireland General Certificate of Education, but often only as an optional course and always confined to the twentieth century, that is, the birth and history of the Northern Ireland state. One example of what this instruction produces, and also of the difficulties a teacher faces if he or she tries to break out of it, is given in the following dialogue between a history teacher and a Protestant pupil, recorded in 1970:

> When a pupil pointed to a Celtic cross on a classroom wall I was asked:
> 'Sir, what's that fenian cross doing on our wall?'
> 'It's not a fenian cross, it's the type of cross the Irish erected when there was no such thing as fenians and prods.'
> 'What do you mean, sir, no such thing as fenians and prods?'
> 'Everybody in those days was a member of the Irish Church.'

61

'The Church [Anglican] of Ireland, sir?'
'No, actually it was the Catholic church.'
'You mean the Catholics ruled Ulster?'
'No, in fact the English ruled Ulster.'
'And they were Protestant?'
'No, everybody was Catholic in those days.'
'So the fenians did rule Ulster.'[26]

There is a reverse side of the coin in the teaching of history. Catholic children are told again and again of the barbarisms of the English, of the way they tried to destroy the Irish Catholic religion, of the heretical English kings. The difference between the two versions is not that one does and one does not try to create its own mythology, but that the portrayals of English barbarism in Ireland do happen to have a vigorous link with reality, and the assertion that Northern Ireland Catholics have been treated as second-class citizens does happen to be true.

This is true in a more general way. The Catholics of Belfast may believe that all Protestants are bound to burn in purgatory or wherever, but the all-pervading self-righteousness of the Protestants does not exist on the Catholic side. The local republican newspapers of recent years do not contain the bigotry and sectarianism of the Protestant papers, and if there is prejudice it is more likely to be directed against the English than at fellow-citizens, and even the most obdurate of historians would admit there is a good deal of justification for that. Catholic working-class newspapers simply do not project themselves as wishing to dominate Protestants: no mention in them of wishing to kill Prod scum, no caricature of Protestants as dirty, smelly and idle.

It is not the intention of this book to compare and contrast the Catholics and Protestants of Northern Ireland, but a small example taken from the opinion poll quoted earlier is interesting. The question was asked if the respondent was in favour of a closer relationship between the Catholic and Protestant churches. Seventy-eight per cent of Catholics replied in the affirmative, but only 34 per cent of members of the Church of Ireland said yes and only 28 per cent of Presbyterians. Those who prided themselves on being part of the ascendency had no wish to bring in others; those who judged themselves God's people had no wish to petition the Almighty to extend his favours. The Protestants are either too sure of themselves or too scared of the outside world to engage in dialogue. Their dialogue was and is the old one, the dialogue of the Orange drum which beats out 'No Surrender', the dialogue of the graveyard.

Even graveyards occasionally witness smiles, and once in a while the working-class Protestant can catch a glimpse of himself. The following joke is taken from another of the contemporary loyalist newspapers, one that is usually little better or worse than any of the rest:

> Two neighbours, one Protestant and the other a Catholic, went on holiday together. One had a small son, the other a daughter, neither child had a bathing suit, but as the beach was remote the parents allowed them to paddle naked. Afterwards when the wee boy was being dried by his mother he remarked, 'Mother, I never knew there was so much difference between Catholics and Protestants.'[27]

Such jokes are very few and far between in the loyalist newspapers. They are more likely to write about 'fenian scum' or suggest that burning down houses and the people inside them is an acceptable way of getting rid of 'all the shit'. There is nothing very amusing in that, so it is easier to laugh at the Protestants than with them; easier to laugh at the spectacle of the poorly paid and badly housed strutting about in Orange demonstrations imagining they are enjoying some far-reaching privilege. But that too would be misplaced. There is little to laugh at in a community which, however farcical it might appear, considers itself to be a chosen people.

5

Lundies

The Orange culture has produced very few good songs. Craven papists, Orange victories, fenian blood and Protestant supremacy run through them all with a predictability and repetitiveness of a Lambeg drum. Even the melodies tend to be tedious or unoriginal, based as most of them are on either Gaelic Irish or Scottish tunes. But there are exceptions, and they are occasionally amusing with a strong narrative line. Such a song is 'The Ould Orange Flute', which tells the tales of one Bob Williamson, a 'stout Orange blade' and flute-player in a Protestant band. The song relates how 'Bob the deceiver' married a Catholic and 'turned papish himself', as a result of which 'the boys in the town made some noise upon it', and Bob fled to the dark and dreary papish south. Bob took the 'ould Orange flute' and the song tells how the flute was Bob's downfall. When he tried to play it for a Catholic choir,

> The instrument shivered and sighed, Oh Alas,
> When he blew it and fingered and made a great noise,
> The flute would play only 'The Protestant Boys'.

Whenever Bob tried to play 'papish music', only good Protestant songs thundered forth. In the end the flute was 'burned as heretic', but,

> While the flames roared around it they heard a
>   great noise,
> T'was the ould flute still playing 'The Protestant
>   Boys'.

An amusing and harmless enough song, often performed by republican as well as Orange balladeers, it illustrates one of the strongest threads in loyalism – the warning not to go over to the other side. The most hated character in Orange history is not some fiendish rebel, or devil-worshipping communist agitator, but one Robert Lundy, the Protestant governor of Londonderry, who in 1689 attempted to surrender the city to the Catholic King James II, rather than wait for the arrival of the glorious Protestant King William III. For the Ulster Protestant the name Lundy has become synonymous with traitors and turncoats. To be a 'lundy' is the capital crime of Ulster loyalism, worse even than being a 'fenian lover', a phrase of more recent coinage.

What could be described as a more positive aspect of this attitude is the call to unity within the loyalist camp. 'The Price of Liberty is Eternal Vigilance' is a well-worn loyalist slogan, alerting the faithful not just to the Catholic masses waiting to sack the house of Orange, but to those inside who knowingly or unknowingly may open the gates to the enemy. Within the gates loyalism demands unanimity; 'United We Stand, Divided We Fall' has been an election slogan of the Unionist Party, and is to be found painted on the tenement walls and embroidered on Orange banners. It has served the political masters of Northern Ireland well on the few occasions that their rule resulted in murmurs of discontent from the loyalist ranks. In the 1918 general election when the upper-class Unionists were challenged by several independent unionists, Carson wrote a personal letter to each saying: 'I am most anxious to avoid any appearance of disunion in our ranks at this critical election.'[1] In 1938, when James Craig was faced with the best organised and most extensive unionist opposition to the official party, he countered: 'I would appeal with all the earnestness at my command for a closing of the ranks against the common enemy.'[2] Similarly in the 1949 election, when Brooke met a determined challenge from independent unionist and Labour candidates he rallied: 'differences of opinion on domestic matters must not divide us. Loyalists must stand united.'[3]

Not only has the Unionist leadership called for unity in general, it has taken care to raise the spectre of the common enemy whenever the Protestants started quarrelling amongst themselves. Elections have been called to coincide with times when the Catholic threat could be portrayed as at its height: in 1938, when the twenty-six county state adopted a new constitution which claimed Northern Ireland as part of its territory; in 1949, on the heels of the declaration of the Irish Republic and its quitting the British Commonwealth. On each such occasion partition and union with Britain were presented as the election issue and a judgement on the economic policies of the ruling party was avoided.

Until the 1969 election, when the leader of the Unionist Party, Terence O'Neill, actually campaigned against candidates of his own party, the tactic worked. There were some shaky moments, though. There is a considerable history of rebellion against the Unionist leadership from within the loyalist camp. Broadly speaking, the rebellion has taken two forms, one adopting such labels as Independent Unionist, Progressive Unionist or Democratic Unionist, the other placing itself in the tradition of social democracy – Labour Representation Committee, Independent Labour Party or Northern Ireland Labour Party. Neither has been successful, but their existence suggests that it would be unfair and unhistorical to judge the Protestant lower classes solely by the words and actions of the Unionist Party. The right of the gentry and millionaires to speak for the loyalist workers has been challenged – to be sure, by a minority, unsuccessfully – and the challengers have been termed 'lundies' by the Unionist establishment.

The Ulster Unionist Labour Association, first formed in 1918 and still retaining a paper existence, might seem to be one such group. Established at a time of considerable trade-union militancy in Belfast and elsewhere in Northern Ireland (see chapter 6), the UULA described itself as 'an association of workers formed to support and maintain the legislative union';[4] that is, a separate and distinctly working-class organisation within the general

66

framework of Unionism. In fact the UULA was no such thing. In conception and organisation it owed most to John Andrews, a wealthy industrialist and one of the leading figures in the Unionist Party, later to be a Northern Ireland Prime Minister; its first president was none other than Edward Carson, who had voted against every measure of trade-union and social reform during his parliamentary career (see chapter 3). The truth is that it was no more than a Unionist Party front dreamed up by the Unionist establishment occasionally to contest elections in working-class areas. Its politics were made plain by Andews at one of the organisation's rallies: 'employees would recognise that capital was a necessity and that a controlling influence was a requisite for the successful conduct of every industry and enterprise.'[5]

There have, it is true, been a few genuine workers in the organisation, most prominently William Grant, who contested numerous elections for the Unionists in the inter-war years. But they have been rather peculiar animals even for the working-class Protestant. Grant, for example, played a leading part in an organisation called 'The Bible Standards League', and presided on one occasion at a meeting held to protest against, 'modernism in the Presbyterian sabbeth school book'.[6] 'As to the rent question', he once commented,

> I believe that the landlords are entitled to justice equally with their tenants, but if there are any means whereby increases in rent could be avoided without doing injustice to either of the parties concerned, I am prepared to use any influence I might possess in the Ulster parliament to secure that result.[7]

The UULA can be brushed aside as irrelevant, and was certainly inconsequential in 1974; in its own words, 'the main event of our year was the Ulster Unionist Council and the Association combining to have a wreath-laying memorial service for Lord Carson, [when we] heard a stirring speech from the Rt Hon. Enoch Powell.'[8] But the Association illustrates a further way in which the Unionist establishment seeks to head off any opposition from the

67

Protestant ranks, in this case by setting up their own 'workers' organisation. As always, the loyal workers were rewarded with a few crumbs, for the UULA are allowed 20 delegates to the annual meeting of the Unionist Council, not very many compared to the Orange Order's 122, but something all the same.

There have been genuine oppositions within the loyalist community, and while it is unnecessary to detail each individual contest it is important to get a flavour of what they stood for and how they fared. The first rumblings of protest came from the agricultural lower classes, for although the Tory Land Act of 1885 provided funds for tenants to purchase the land they worked, the sale of estates was neither universal nor compulsory. By the turn of the century discontent was mounting amongst the rural poor and T. W. Russell, himself a leading Unionist, was questioning the motives of his political colleagues:

> I thought that the Irish landlords were Unionist on high political grounds, that they were fighting for their country's good not their own. I do not think that today. On the contrary I have come to the conclusion that in pretending to fight for the Union these men are simply fighting for their own interests – that rent not patriotism was their guiding motive.[9]

That was in 1901. In 1902 an independent candidate standing on a platform of universal and compulsory purchase won a by-election in the normally safe Unionist seat of East Down, and in the 1906 general election Russell and two of his followers, all standing as independent Unionists, defeated three official Unionist candidates. However the victory was short-lived and in the following 1910 general election the Unionists regained two of the three seats, including Russell's.

There were three reasons for the collapse of the 'Russellites'. First, the passing of the Wyndham Land Act of 1903 extended facilities for tenant purchase and so dampened the protests. Second, the 1910 election was fought with Home Rule a real possibility and the official Unionists could use the occasion for another, particularly effective, call to close the Protestant ranks.

Third, Russell and his followers were subjected to a campaign of vilification and misrepresentation which all independent Unionists had to undergo whenever they challenged the establishment party. A typical example is found in the *Belfast News-Letter*'s coverage of the January 1910 election:

> The Russellites and the nationalists have at last found a candidate to oppose Mr C. C. Craig [official Unionist] in South Antrim. Mr W. M. Clow has consented to be the anti-Unionist standard bearer though we suppose he will try and persuade the electors that his success will not imperil the Union. But he has been supported by the Russellite faction and the nationalists will endorse his candidature so he must be a Home Ruler no matter what he says or thinks.[9]

All of which was pure nonsense, for the Russellites were as loyalist as any of the official Unionists. Indeed many of the independent Unionists who have contested elections in the last seventy-odd years thought the official party's Unionism to be suspect. When one of the leading independents of the inter-war years, W. J. Stewart, was accused of endangering the Union by standing against the party, he replied: 'The danger of the Union today lies in those men who are endeavouring to retain the old privileges and their ascendency and who are thus connecting the Union with privilege and ascendency.'[11] Stewart had a long and varied career against official Unionism. The comment quoted above was made in 1918, when he was standing against a Carson-backed candidate in a Protestant working-class constituency. He was defeated in that election but successful in 1929, when he was elected to Westminster as an independent Unionist. In 1938 he organised the most widespread challenge to official Unionism that had been seen when he formed the Progressive Unionist Party, which contested ten seats in the Northern Ireland parliamentary elections. He was again accused of aiding the forces of Irish nationalism and again he replied dismissively:

> Partition as an election cry has no value because all Unionists in Northern Ireland are firmly opposed to any attempt to interfere

with the province as an integral part of the United Kingdom. . . .
We will fight the election on the question of unemployment.[12]

Stewart's attempt to introduce an element of class politics into Northern Ireland met with failure: all ten of his candidates were defeated. But neither he nor Russell before him were political freaks dealing in something alien to the Protestant lower classes. There was a whole series of such candidates in the first half of the twentieth century; some of them were successful, all of them impatient with the results of official Unionism:

> They talked about the freedom of Ulster, but where was it? They might have heard of Tammany Hall, New York, where no man could get a job unless he was recommended. They had the same thing here only worse. When they elected a member for parliament he was supposed – and said he was going to do so – to represent the people, but instead of that he became one of their rulers, not a representative at all. They were simply electing another boss and he in turn was bossed by another boss and the three little bosses at the top ran the whole show.[13]

P. J. Woods, who made that statement, did so in 1923 in the course of a by-election in west Belfast in which he defeated the official Unionist and Belfast County Grand Master of the Orange Order, Sir Joseph Davison, by nearly 8,000 votes. West Belfast is an evenly balanced Catholic/Protestant constituency, but it is fair to estimate that Woods captured at least a third of the Protestant vote in that election. As with other independents, Woods' success was short-lived. He was a victim of the changes in electoral law which Craig introduced in 1929 (see chapter 7).

An independent Unionist who escaped that fate was Tom Henderson. Henderson was first elected in the general election of 1925 by the solidly working-class Protestant constituency of Shankill and represented it in the Northern Ireland Parliament for nearly thirty years. He was careful to declare he was not a socialist, only 'a friend of the worker',[14] but he did in general seek to raise and agitate on the bread-and-butter issues which any conventional social democrat would find himself involved with. His main issues in the 1925 election campaign were higher old age pensions and more government expenditure in housing;[15] in 1932 he was heavily involved in the unemployment agitation (see chapter 7).

The fact that Henderson was elected again and again makes his Shankill Road constituents seem less the reactionary Orangemen and willing lapdogs of the Orange bosses they are often made out to be. On the other hand an area such as the Shankill, one of the most deprived in Belfast, would have returned a much more left-wing candidate anywhere other than in Northern Ireland. It is also true that the Protestant lower classes have not produced or responded to any general move to dislodge the Unionist establishment, such as has come from the political Labour movement.

That movement too has had its successes. Three Labour candidates were elected in the Northern Ireland election of 1925, one in 1929, two in 1933, in 1938 and in 1945. Their greatest victory came in 1958 when four Northern Ireland Labour Party candidates were elected to Stormont. Generally speaking the Labour candidates' election campaigns concentrated on bread-and-butter issues, 'municipal socialism' as William Walker, a founding father of the Belfast Labour movement, described it.[16] The Labour candidates invariably supported the Union, but as they also drew attention to the miserable social and economic conditions over which the Unionist establishment presided, they earned the usual abuse and misrepresentation. Thus in 1920 when Labour won 13 seats on the Belfast corporation, Edward Carson intervened to warn his followers about the 'Bolshevik–Sinn Fein alliance' and went on to declare:

> What I say is this: these men who come forward posing as friends of labour care no more about labour than does the man in the moon. Their real object and the real insidious object of their propaganda is to mislead and bring about disunity among our own people and in the end, before we know it, we may find ourselves in the same bondage and slavery as in the rest of Ireland, in the south and west.[17]

It would be an insult to the intelligence of the Protestant working class to explain Labour's lack of success as a product of these slanders. The reason for their failure to attract popular support is more complicated and will be examined in the concluding chapter of this book. But for all the exaggeration and the misrepresentation it is true that the Union was not the single major priority for them and they could be dismissed as an irrelevancy whenever the national question became, or was presented as being, the key issue: thus, while the NILP grew from the mid 1950s onwards, once the national question re-emerged in the 1970s, Labour was reduced to the status of observers, gaining only one seat in the 72-seat Convention of 1975. At the same time, their Unionism always imposed strict limitations on their politics of reform, since there was the real possibility that they would go the whole hog and accept the entire Orange philosophy. A living example of this process is David Bleakley, the leading figure of the NILP for the last ten years, who in 1971 accepted an appointment as Minister for Community Relations in Brian Faulkner's first cabinet, although he was not an MP and although, more significantly, his appointment provided a 'left cover' for Faulkner. Perhaps Bleakley's intentions were honourable, a desire to bring a degree of non-partisanship to the Unionist establishment, but as Faulkner's policies of internment, repression and torture were put into practice it became as clear as day that it was Bleakley who had been captured by Faulkner, not the other way around.

Harry Midgley is another example. One of the leaders of Northern Ireland Labour in the 1930s and 1940s, Midgley ended up in a Unionist cabinet and in 1949 stood as an official Unionist. However, the most important example by far is that of William Walker, the ideological Godfather of Northern Ireland Labour.

Walker was never elected to a national parliament – he died in 1918 before the Northern Ireland state was established. But his 'socialism' has left a deep mark on Labour politics in Northern Ireland. In spite of electoral defeats he had a successful career. He was President of the Irish TUC, secretary of the Belfast Trades

Council, member of the executive of the British Labour Party and member of the Belfast corporation. But Walker's major claim to fame is his polemic with James Connolly. The controversy began with his refusal to support an all-Ireland Labour Party, preferring instead to form an Irish branch of the British-based Independent Labour Party. The discussion between him and Connolly soon involved much more than that and centred around the attitude socialists should adopt to the link with Britain. Connolly was in no doubt, describing the ILP as, 'scarcely distinguishable from imperialism, the merging of a subjected people into the political system of their conquerors.'[17] To this Walker gave two replies. One was that 'everything the people of Ireland want can be safeguarded under the protection of the United Democracies (UK),'[18] and the second, that Belfast had made greater advances towards what Walker thought to be socialism than Dublin:

> We collectively own and control our gas works, water works, harbour works, markets, tramways, electricity, museums, art galleries, etc., whilst we municipally cater for bowlers, cricketers, footballers, lovers of band music (having organised a police band).[19]

Connolly preferred not to argue over the practical achievements of 'gas and water socialism' but rather to emphasise the implications and nature of Walker's creed, which Connolly insisted allied itself with Orangeism. As proof Connolly cited Walker's response to a number of questions he had been asked in a 1905 by-election. The following are some of the questions and Walker's replies:

> Q: Would you resist every effort to throw open the offices of the Lord Chancellor of England and Lord Lieutenant of Ireland to Roman Catholics?
> Walker: Yes.
> Q: Will you contend against every proposal to open diplomatic relations between the Vatican and the Court of St James?
> Walker: Yes.

Q: Will you resist every attack upon the legislative enactments provided by our forefathers as necessary safeguards against the encroachment of the Papacy?

Walker: Yes.[20]

Because of this sectarianism Connolly declared himself pleased that Walker was defeated in the by-election, reasoning that had he been successful and elected as a socialist, socialists would have been subjected to 'an inveterate hatred of the cause . . . wherever Irishmen live and work'.[21]

The Connolly/Walker controversy was to be remembered in the early 1970s when a similar debate took place within the Irish left. The NILP adopted Walker's position, arguing as he did that the over-riding need was to unite Protestant and Catholic workers on bread-and-butter issues. The NILP tried to do it, in their half-hearted way, and are helplessly preaching from the sidelines. They could not read the record, even though it was printed in blood. In 1911 William Walker wrote: 'I affirm that it has now become impossible in Belfast to have a religious riot and this is due to the good work done by that much despised body, the ILP.'[22]

The following year there were widespread sectarian riots. The influence of Walker's work was seen in the results of the elections to the Belfast corporation in 1920. That same year a prolonged and large-scale sectarian war broke out in Belfast. Nearly 300 people died, mostly Catholics.

While Walker was leading socialism in Belfast along a religiously sectarian path, an attempt was being made in the opposite direction – to pull Protestant sectarianism along the path of Irish self-determination. This was true lundyism, a real break with tradition, led by Lindsay Crawford, who wrote:

Our faith in British honour has been shaken and we can no longer pretend that we are enamoured of the English connection. English rule in Ireland stands self-condemned. What has English rule in Ireland brought Protestants? Are they satisfied to be treated as the oddments and remnants of the British constitution in Ireland?[23]

74

Or:

> The Act of Union was carried by corruption and bribery and it is no exaggeration to say that by the same despicable methods has the Act of Union been best maintained . . . The Act of Union was being maintained in this country under conditions prejudicial to the best interests of Ireland.[24]

Crawford's heresies appeared in the columns of the *Irish Protestant*, a paper he founded in 1901 and which he edited until 1906. The paper was printed in Dublin, although Crawford himself came from a northern Protestant background and addressed the paper primarily to the Protestants of the north. It was a well-produced newspaper and, judging by the extensive advertising it carried, it had a healthy circulation.

But what gave Crawford a special significance was his relationship with Tom Sloan, an independent Unionist for South Belfast elected in a by-election in 1902. Sloan stood because he thought the official Unionist candidate, Charles Dunbar-Buller, had been selected undemocratically. He ran his campaign on typical Protestant populist lines: he accused the official Unionists of being soft on Catholicism, instancing their Westminster votes against the inspection of convent laundries; at the same time he attacked the 'deadheads' of Ulster Unionism and advocated trade-union rights and old age pensions. The Belfast Trades Council, possibly because of Walker's influence, supported Sloan as a labour-minded candidate, despite his bigotry.

Sloan was suspended from the Orange Order after the election and in June 1903 formed the breakaway Independent Orange Order with Lindsay Crawford as its Grand Master. The direction which Crawford hoped to see the new organisation take was indicated at the founding meeting:

> The Prime Minister himself represents a decaying class, out of touch with the people, out of touch with the genius of progress – a class which would not be tolerated in any community of thinking men, because it represents the spirit of retrogression and surrender.[25]

The IOO was an immediate success. Its first demonstration attracted 500 people and on the 12 July parade of 1904 2,000 marched behind its banner. During these opening years Crawford used the *Irish Protestant* to egg on his followers towards a complete break with the Orange tradition. He shared the populism of Sloan and other independents before and since: he attacked the 'bloated plutocrats' of the Unionist establishment, a phrase he used on many occasions; and supported the campaign for women's suffrage. More distinctively, he moved towards Home Rule. In July 1905, at a meeting at Maghermore, County Antrim, the IOO issued a new manifesto which attacked clericalism, called for compulsory land purchase, urged a revision of Irish finances, accused English Liberals and Tories of playing Protestant and Catholic off against each other, and concluded:

> We consider it is high time that the Irish Protestants consider their position as Irish citizens and their attitudes towards their Roman Catholic countrymen and that the latter should choose once and for all between nationality and sectarianism. In an Ireland in which Protestant and Catholic stand sullen and discontented it is not too much to hope that they will recognise their position and in their common trials unite on a basis of nationality . . . There is room in Ireland for a patriotic party which will devote itself to the task of freeing the country from the domination of impractical creeds and organised tyrannies and to securing the urgent and legitimate redress of her many grievances.[26]

The Maghermore Manifesto, as it became known, went well beyond the standard protests of independent Unionism. Yet there was no immediate mutiny in the ranks and one branch of the old Orange Order even adopted it. The radical nationalist, Michael Davitt (see chapter 8), added his praise, in a sense returning the compliment for Crawford's many commendations in the *Irish Protestant*.

Not all of the springs of this new part of Orangeism were pure. While Sloan's election success flowed from his attacks on the 'Ulster deadheads', some of it came from his attacks from the right.

As Crawford explained,

> Between 1901 and July 1902 the government had aroused a storm of opposition in Irish Protestant circles. The attempt to tamper with the Royal Declaration, the exclusion of convent laundries from the Workshops Act ... and the squeezing out of the Protestant minority all over the country bore fruit in the revolt of a number of Ulster Orangemen, which culminated in the return of Tom Sloan and the split in the Orange institution.[27]

There is, in the suspicion that the established leaders were selling out the Protestant cause, an obvious resemblance to the sentiments which gave rise to Paisleyism (see chapter 3). Equally there were times when the *Irish Protestant* carried the kind of material which now fills the pages of Paisley's *Protestant Telegraph*. Even Paisley's paranoia had an equivalent in headlines like 'Is Methodism Heading Towards Romanism?' But Crawford was no Paisley. Addressing himself to Catholics he proclaimed: 'At every important crisis in your history the cause of nationality has been bartered by your priest for increased clerical power.'[28] From this he concluded: 'Both the British government and the Church of Rome have proved to be implacable foes of Irish nationality.'[29] So while Paisley and his like see Irish nationalism as, to quote a phrase of William Walker, 'handing Ireland over to the domination of the priesthood',[30] Crawford argued from the opposite direction saying that 'our determined stand against priestly power and tyranny is justified on national grounds'.[31]

Crawford made much use of 'national grounds' and similar euphemisms. During his editorship of the *Irish Protestant* he never explicitly stated that he was in favour of Irish Home Rule, although he came very close, as when he wrote, 'the great blunder has been made in the past by the Irish Protestant that England and not Ireland has been his native country'.[32] In addition he lent support to ostensibly non-political aspects of Irish nationalism such as the propagation of Irish language and culture through the Gaelic League. But the *Irish Protestant* never completely embraced the

Irish national cause. Perhaps Crawford feared his audience's reaction; perhaps it was because the new Ireland he sought would be incomplete without the participation of the Protestant minority. As he said in summary, at a time when his influence was declining,

> It is not by opposing the ideals of government, but by directing the hopes and ambitions of the country towards them that the evils most dreaded under Home Rule will be averted. It is not by denouncing the abstract principle of self-government – which has passed into law in our colonies and dependencies – that the Union between England and Ireland will be best preserved, but by educating the people of Ireland to the level of self-government. And Ireland will only be ripe for self-government when, from the North and South, our people stand for the rule of the people, as opposed to the rule of the clergy and when Irish nationality presents no barriers to the progress of democracy.[33]

Clearly Crawford did not support the advanced republican wing of the Irish national movement. He continued to affirm that whatever the degree of Home Rule in Ireland a link with the British Empire should be preserved. Yet in a sense this makes Crawford all the more significant. He was not simply one of the rather rare breed of Protestant nationalist; he always interpreted his nationalism through Protestant, at times Orange, eyes. Like the rest of the Protestant camp he saw in Irish Protestantism a moral supremacy, arguing that 'the higher commercial and social status of the Protestants is due solely to the merits of Protestantism'.[34] But Crawford's very exceptional brand of Orangeism attempted to abstract from the general ideology whatever atoms of progressivism it contained and move them towards Irish self-determination.

It hardly needs to be said that the attempt failed. Sloan disavowed the Maghermore Manifesto just before the 1906 general election and in the same year Crawford was forced out of the editorship of the *Irish Protestant*. He was eventually expelled from the IOO for being a Home Ruler. His fate, in a uniquely favourable period when discontent with the Unionist leadership coincided with trade-union militancy in Belfast, tells much about the hold of Orange culture and about attempts to reform Orangeism from within. A strategy of moving 'progressive' elements of the Orange ideology towards a non-sectarian Irish radicalism contains too many contradictions, is built on too many illusions. Nothing that has happened since Lindsay Crawford has given flesh to those illusions.

As for Crawford himself, like Bob Williamson, the anti-hero of the song quoted at the start of this chapter, he 'fled'. He left for Canada in 1908 and eventually became a representative of the Irish Free State in New York. Just what the 'Ould Orange Flute' would have thought of that is not for the ears of the young and innocent.

6

The Workers

The General Strike of 1926 is the great historical occasion of the British working class; nine days which summed up its experience and its attitudes. Solidarity and defeat; reaching for power and retreat. It is the memory-bank of the British trade-union militant which contains a lesson of special significance. There was no way it could have ended but in total victory or in total defeat. The controversy remains, the recriminations remain, the defeat remains.

The General Strike occurred just five years after the Protestant community in north-east Ireland, made powerful by the presence of the Protestant working class, had fought and won their victory to remain British. Many arguments had been used to achieve that success, including William Walker's that there was an indissoluble link between the British and Irish labour movements. Yet at the time of the strike the Belfast branch of the British-based Railway Clerks Association received the following telegram: 'It is not felt necessary to call upon the membership in Ireland, the Channel Islands, Antwerp or Brussels to join the strike.'[1] That Belfast was considered as remote as Belgium, during the greatest single struggle of the British working class, was not a reflection of some anti-Irish sentiment, or of ignorance on the part of the English-based trade union. It was an opinion held equally strongly in Northern Ireland. As Sam Kyle, a leading figure in the Belfast labour and trade-union movement said at the time, 'Heaven forbid the trade-union movement in Northern Ireland would take our stand with our comrades across the water.'[2]

Kyle's fears were never realised. The only action Northern Ireland workers took during the General Strike was the blacking by dockers in Belfast and Derry of goods from and for Great Britain. Even that solitary action was no indication of the 'Britishness' of the Northern Ireland trade-union movement, for dockers in Waterford, Drogheda and Dublin in the 'Irish' part of Ireland took the same steps.[3]

One inference that can be drawn from the 1926 story is that there is little sense of identity between the trade unions in Northern Ireland and Great Britain. A second, more important one is that the two labour movements should be judged separately, with the aid of different norms. In Britain, the key to working-class struggles is in the history of the trade-union movement; in Ireland this is not true. 'Economic' issues – wages, conditions, trade-union rights and so on – have not assumed the prominence of the over-riding political question, namely the presence of Britain in Ireland. In consequence the official trade-union movement in Northern Ireland does not speak with the same authority as its counterpart in Great Britain. To take a recent example, the 1974 Northern Ireland General Strike against power-sharing and the Council of Ireland was opposed by all the official trade-union organisations in Northern Ireland, indeed all of Ireland. A 'Back to Work' march designed to break the strike, although sponsored by the Irish Congress of Trade Unions, supported by the Belfast Trades Council and led by the General Secretary of the British Trade Union Congress, attracted less than 200 people. The great body of Protestant trade unionists rejected the official leadership and showed by their absence that the trade-union movement was of no relevance in the existing political crisis.

The history of the trade-union movement in Northern Ireland divides easily into two parts – before and after Partition – and centres on Belfast, its industrial heart. Even before Partition it had developed differently from the British movement. While the latter experienced something of an internal revolution from the 1880s onwards, when 'new unionism' began to spread among the unskilled, the same process did not take place in Belfast until ten years later. Since the skilled workers in Belfast were over-whelmingly Protestants (see chapter 2), this meant that the trade-union movement was at first largely confined to Protestants. It was not until 1907, with the arrival in Belfast of Jim Larkin, that the north of Ireland really saw what new unionism meant in practice.

Larkin was born in Liverpool in 1876, the son of a northern Irish father, and came to Belfast in 1907 as a full-time organiser for the National Union of Dock Labourers. He hit Belfast like a clenched fist. Within a couple of months he had organised the majority of dockers into the NUDL and displaced the moderate Carters' Association. In June he called out 500 dockers in support of a wage claim. The following month the carters struck in sympathy and put forward demands of their own for a pay rise and the right to operate a closed shop. To these groups were added over the 12 July weekend workers at coal merchants, who were denied the right to organise and were locked out in the wake of the general agitation; even the Royal Irish Constabulary came out for better pay and conditions.

Both Catholic and Protestant trade unionists were involved in the strikes, and radicals of all descriptions rushed to Larkin's side. From the Protestant side, Lindsay Crawford and Tom Sloan spoke at meetings in support of Larkin as did, for a short period, the nationalist leader, Joe Devlin, although he later disassociated himself (see chapter 8). Naturally the employers attempted to stir up sectarian divisions by stressing that Larkin was a Catholic. Larkin offered to resign the leadership of the strikes, but Alexander Boyd, a Protestant trade unionist, replied that all efforts at divide and rule 'would not be successful because men of all creeds are determined to stand together in fighting the common enemy who denied the right of workers to a fair wage'.[4] The employers brought in troops who, in early August, assisted in the arrest of the police leaders and transferred other members of the RIC to outlying districts throughout Ireland. Some of the other strikers fared rather better. The coal dispute was settled in late July with the workers preserving their right to organise, and in mid-August the carters won a wage increase, although their attempt to implement a closed shop failed. Only the dockers suffered total defeat, contributed to by the union leadership in England, who denounced Larkin and his methods.

The results of the 1907 strikes was not as important as the way they were conducted. Larkin was able to introduce a militant spirit into sections of the Belfast working class. The unity he forged seemed to augur well for the future. For all that, there were special circumstances which made the militancy possible. The strikes followed on the heels of the 1906 general election which had seen some form of working-class political unity with Devlin, Walker and Sloan all being supported by the Belfast Trades Council, and they occurred when Home Rule was not an immediate issue. A more substantial test for the potential for trade-union unity between the two working-class communities came in 1911 with the arrival in Belfast of James Connolly.

By then the tussle between Larkin and his trade-union bosses in England had ended with Larkin forming his own Irish Transport and General Workers' Union, and it was as a branch secretary of that union that Connolly came to Belfast in June. He came with over twenty years of activity in the Irish and international socialist movement behind him. He had already proved himself to be an able agitator and a considerable theoretician, and had emerged on the left wing of the international socialist movement during debates within the Second International. His revolutionary marxism was to be strikingly confirmed in 1914 when he was one of the few European socialists to brand the first world war an imperialist war. Connolly remains, through his writings, his activity and his political programme, the greatest marxist these islands have produced. But in 1911 he was some distance from such fame and, unlike Larkin, he came to Belfast when the antagonism between the two sections of the working class was at one of its periodic peaks. The results of the 1910 general election had made the Liberals dependent for their majority in the House of Commons on the Irish nationalist vote and Home Rule was once again in the offing. It was not an opportune time to repeat Larkin's successes at class unity.

The repeat performance never came. Connolly did have isolated triumphs: soon after he arrived he brought out the largely Catholic deep-sea dockers in sympathy with the predominantly Protestant cross-channel seamen, and he managed to arrange the unusual spectacle of a nonsectarian 'labour band' parading through the streets. But those were minor gains. In attempting to swim against the tide Connolly encountered too strong a sectarian current. One example, the Larne aluminium strike in 1913, illustrates the difficulties.

When Connolly organised the predominantly Protestant aluminium workers into the Irish TGWU it inevitably involved a strike for recognition. The following Sunday the strikers were invited to stay behind after the normal church service whereupon they received a sermon from the clergy on the evil of their actions, and, more important, on the 'Irishness' of Connolly's union. The strike was nothing but a Papish plot. Next day the men returned to work and proved to Connolly that 'the north-east corner of Ulster is the only "priest ridden" part of Ireland.'[5]

The Larne strike was one of the few occasions on which Connolly managed, even temporarily, to attract Protestants to the ITGWU. The fact that Catholics rather than Protestants tended to be in the unskilled class that Connolly was appealing to was not the only problem. When Larkin complained that Connolly was not unifying the working class as successfully as he had, Connolly wrote to another ITGWU official, William O'Brien: 'He [Larkin] is forever snarling at me and drawing comparisons between what he accomplished in Belfast in 1907 and what I have done, conveniently ignoring the fact that he was then Secretary of an *English* organisation.'[6] Fair comment, for as the Larne strike had shown, the fact that Connolly's union had 'Irish' in its title created difficulties. On one occasion Connolly's members were physically attacked at a railway station for no other reason than their membership of an 'Irish' trade union. A further problem arose because Connolly's activities in organising and seeking improvement for lower-paid workers threatened the craft differentials enjoyed by Protestant workers, as became evident when he tried to organise the women workers in Belfast's linen mills.

The main union in the linen mills was the Textile Operatives' Society, under the leadership of Mary Galway, which had been originally set up by the Belfast Trades Council. The union recruited only craft workers, the vast majority of whom were Protestant, and refused to have anything to do with the unskilled girls when they came out on strike. Connolly organised them into the ITGWU. The strike ended in compromise, but hostility grew between Galway and Connolly, who was reported to the Belfast Trades Council for poaching members. Although Galway withdrew the charge later there was no hiding the continued antipathy the Protestant craft workers felt towards their fellow-workers, the unskilled Catholics.

The last major event in the development of trade unionism in pre-Partition Belfast was the strike of shipyard and engineering workers early in 1919. The dispute was part of a general British stoppage on the issue of working hours. The men involved were mainly Protestant, although the leader of the strike committee was a Catholic. The strike was handicapped from the start by not having the support of the Federation of Engineering and Shipping Trades and because the two main unions involved, the Amalgamated Society of Engineers and the Boilermakers' Union, did not give strike pay. It was therefore all the more important for the strikers to accept support from whatever quarter it was offered. But no. An ITGWU offer of sympathy action by shipyard workers was turned down, and the strike ended with an interim settlement when troops were sent in as strike-breakers. Eighteen months later, after the Belfast shipyards had gone through the most vicious outbreak of sectarian violence it had ever experienced, the men accepted the settlement as final. The violence was to spread and intensify, and the following year the shipyard workers, their minds on other matters, accepted a wage cut.

The 1919 strike was the last great clash between employers and organised labour in Belfast. There have been many other disputes since but nothing again reached the proportions of 1907 or 1919. Trade-union militancy was suspended during the sectarian violence of 1920 and has yet to be renewed. A full-page advertisement in English newspapers inserted by the Northern Ireland government in 1973 tells what has happened since. Headed 'Northern Ireland – The Business News' the advertisement was made up of quotes from English and international newspapers and included the following:

> 'Gain their confidence and they will work the hind legs off a donkey', says plant manager William Hill . . . 'Being in Derry is like sitting on a gold mine' – *Sunday Times*

> Autolite Motor Products Ltd, a Ford carburettor factory in Belfast . . . stated that in 1971 it had the top car plant within its group in Europe on the manufacturing budget and, in a year when Ford of Britain had made a loss, had been against the trend, having in fact improved its profits – *Neue Zurcher Zeitung*

> Firms were attracted to Northern Ireland by its exceptional labour record. In 1971 the Province lost only 203 days per 1,000 workers through industrial disputes. The UK lost 719 – *Observer*

> Bridgeport Brass, a subsidiary of the National Distillers and Chemical Corporation which recently took over a British firm, is moving all production to its headquarters in Belfast. In eleven years in Ulster the company claims never to have lost a single day's production. – *US News and World Reports*

> In the field of industrial relations the role of the trade-union movement is of course decisive. In principle this role is the same as anywhere else in the world, but in practice (in Northern Ireland) it works out completely differently to the remainder of Great Britain. Cecil Vance, chairman of the Amalgamated Transport and General Workers Union had this to say: 'Our union has 90,000 members but is independent of the parent organisation in England.

We receive guidelines from Transport House . . . but are able to pursue our own policy. That policy is orientated towards more employment opportunities' – *Elseviers Weekblad*

One of the influences which over the years has encouraged companies to move to Ulster has been the country's labour record. Days lost through stoppages are fewer than one third of the UK average. – *Industry Week*[7]

The advertisement was a nice change both for advertisements and for statements emanating from the Northern Ireland government – it came close to telling the truth. The 1971 strike figures which it paraded for approval were exceptional in only one way – they were the highest in Northern Ireland for thirteen years.[8] Nothing has changed since then: in 1973 days lost in proportion to the working population were again approximately one third of that of the UK as a whole, and an even smaller percentage for that of Scotland and Wales, also areas of high unemployment[9]; far less too than in the twenty-six counties which, despite a similarly high level of unemployment, topped the world 'strike league' a number of times during the 1960s and early 1970s.

The lack of trade-union militancy is not due to general satisfaction with the standard of living: that is much lower than in Great Britain (see chapter 2). Nor is it due to the lack of issues to fight on. Unemployment alone has sparked off mass outbursts, most notably in 1932 (see chapter 7) but also as late as 1963. Even the Civil Rights movement in 1968, while concentrating on discrimination against Catholics, was involved to some extent in agitating for more job opportunities. Nor can the lack of trade-union militancy be blamed on a lack of unionisation, for Northern Ireland has one of the highest levels of trade-union membership in the UK. The explanation for the death of the spirit of 1907 lies elsewhere, and a clue found in the following words of Brian Faulkner, uttered at a meeting of the Orange Order in 1963:

Many a company director has marched with his lodge today, shoulder to shoulder with wage earners. This is a healthy state of affairs. This is the right grounds on which to build the soundest of industrial relations.[10]

As with so much else the explanation in the end comes back to the workings of Ulster Unionism. That the Unionist alliance has been an all-class alliance, that through that alliance the Protestant workers have gained marginal privileges, that within the alliance the Orange Order, controlled by the Unionist establishment, provides a social service for the Protestant worker – all this not only helps to prevent the emergence of class consciousness, it also provides an alternative for the services normally associated with trade unions: a social life, a 'brotherhood', a preservation of a labour aristocracy. Like many other trade unionists, the Protestant trade unionists have been 'bought off', not, however, through the normal channels of industrial disputes and compromises but through a distinct political system; and their craft mentality is sustained, not so much through a form of trade unionism, but through a process of economic and social differentials which has its roots in that political system. And if, on occasions, economic agitation has threatened to disrupt the pattern, the threat has never been carried out. The Unionist establishment has always neutralised it, as they did in 1932 by labelling it a Catholic plot and by promoting, nakedly, a policy of jobs for Protestants first.

Throughout this book Unionist statements are used to illustrate their conscious use of sectarianism for political ends. A further example follows. It was made not in the dark days of the 1930s but in 1961, and it was not spoken by a Unionist 'hardliner' but someone normally associated with the moderate wing of the Unionist party: 'The Unionist Party should make it clear that it is the loyalists who have the first choice of jobs . . . The Unionist Party was founded to further the objects of loyalists.'[11] And just as Ulster Unionism has embraced all Protestants and promised the advancement of all Protestants, so too the ostensible policy of the Unionists – the preservation of the British connection – has been used to relegate other considerations. In an interview held in 1975 with a working-class leader of the Shankill Road Ulster Defence Association, the priorities were stated distinctly:

> Unions are irrelevant in the present situation. We always encourage our men to participate in the unions . . . the main, only reason for getting involved is to try and break away from the Irish Congress of Trade Unions and set up our own Ulster TUC.[12]

The same week as Tommy Lyttle was making that statement, the Orange Order produced its annual programme for the 12 July celebrations which included a section on trade unions. Again there was a plea for participation defending 'the democratic institutions of this country . . . projecting and protecting the ideals of British democracy'. The article continued:

> Do not let the old-fashioned innuendos of class structure and cloth-cap brigade deter you. If you project truth and sincerity when presenting resolutions or defending your way of life you have nothing to fear.[13]

That the Orange Order can talk of anything being 'old-fashioned' is a nice piece of unintentional humour. More important, given its long history of strike-breaking, the fact that it feels able to promote sectarianism in the trade unions (which is what 'defending your way of life' amounts to in Ulster language) demonstrates how confident it is that the trade unions pose not the slightest threat to the Unionist establishment.

The Unionist establishment has not been content with sectarianism and Partition as the only weapons against a united working-class movement. Other devices have been used. The 1927 Trades Disputes and Trade Union Act passed in Britain after the General Strike but later repealed is still in operation in Northern Ireland, limiting the use of unions' political funds and making all sympathy strikes illegal. It was only in 1964 that the Unionist government recognised the Northern Ireland Committee of the Irish Congress of Trade Unions (before 1959 the Irish TUC), the official voice of trade unionism in Northern Ireland. Until then it had argued that, the ICTU being an all-Ireland body, nonrecognition 'arises from the fundamental principle we hold, that of unity with Britain and our rejection of any control from Dublin.'[14] Obviously the existence of a trade-union organisation which attempted, if only on paper, to bridge sectarian differences and unite the working class throughout Ireland was a prospect Ulster Unionism would not view too kindly, but the excuse that the ICTU was controlled from Dublin was not the only consideration. When the Churches' Industrial Council in Northern Ireland attempted to liaise between the ICTU and the government they found that a principal objection of many Unionist backbenchers was not that it was Irish, but that it was a trade-union organisation at all.[15]

The very existence of the ICTU as an all-Ireland organisation, and the fact that the vast majority of Protestant trade unionists are affiliated to it, appears contrary to everything they believe in and work for. Although, as is apparent from the words of Tommy Lyttle quoted above, it is something many Protestant trade unionists are now seeking to correct, it merits an explanation.

The ICTU is a successor to the Irish TUC, formed in 1894. It was set up not for nationalist reasons but in recognition of the fact that Ireland had distinct labour problems and coverage of Irish affairs by the British TUC was minimal. That an early president of the Irish TUC was the constitutional Unionist William Walker reflected on the non-political nature of the organisation.

After Partition the ITUC remained the sovereign body of all trade unionism in Ireland, although the word sovereign implies a degree of authority which never really existed. Its first concrete recognition of the political divisions in Ireland came in 1942 when a Northern Ireland sub-committee of the ITUC was formed. Its first open split on the national question was in 1946, when a number of Irish-based unions broke away from the controlling influence in the ITUC of British-based unions. The split was healed in 1959 when the Irish-based unions were conceded a majority on the executive of what now became the Irish Congress of Trade Unions (the rule was scrapped in 1970).

Since the war the Northern Ireland Committee has become increasingly autonomous, and although in theory it is still only a sub-committee its authority is much more substantial than this implies. It holds its own annual conference, enjoys a good deal of 'home rule' and maintains strong links with the British as well as Irish sovereign trade-union bodies. In this way 'unity' is maintained and a break-up into a Protestant and a Catholic TUC is avoided.

It is a complicated set of arrangements which does little more than paper over the cracks. In reality there are two trade-union worlds. Eighty-four per cent of trade-union members in Northern Ireland belong to the British-based unions compared with 9 per cent in Irish-based unions.[16] Some of them cover the same jobs, trades or professions. In teaching, for example, Protestants are organised in the British-based National Union of Teachers and Catholics in the Irish National Teachers' Organisation.

Not all trades or jobs have a 'Catholic' and a 'Protestant' trade union, and even where Irish and British unions compete their members do not always fall neatly into religious compartments. While there is for example, both an Irish and a British Transport and General Workers' Union, only a relatively small number of workers in Northern Ireland – about 6,500 – belong to the ITGWU, nowhere near the number of Catholics who are eligible. Similarly, almost all bank employees, Protestant and Catholic, belong to an Irish-based union. Probably no more than a quarter or a third of Catholic trade unionists are in Irish unions, although the overwhelming majority of Protestants are in British unions.

Nevertheless, there are close limits on the degree to which trade unions in Northern Ireland can act on the 'brothers at work' formula. Because Protestants tend to occupy the skilled jobs and Catholics are over-represented in the unskilled (see chapter 2), the unions which organise on the basis of skills tend to be segregated on that account alone. It is not that Catholics don't want to join such unions, they are simply not eligible. The fact that there are geographically based union branches adds to the segregation, since they reflect the ghettoised living arrangements. Finally, the membership of the unions at the level of the factory branch or committee reflects the discrimination in public and private industry. For example, it is easy to say that trade unionists of all religions have an opportunity to mix and work together at Sorocco Engineering Works in Belfast; but there are few Catholic trade unionists at Sorocco; there are few Catholics at Sorocco.

Nevertheless the myth of trade-union 'unity' in Northern Ireland remains, and because the ICTU does contain Protestant and Catholic members and because the priority at all times is to preserve that 'unity', whatever moves the ICTU takes to implement basic trade-union principles (such as equality in employment or in housing) are strictly limited. The ICTU cannot go far without losing its Protestant members completely. In 1966 a delegation from the Northern Ireland Committee and the Northern Ireland Labour Party went on a visit to the then Unionist Prime Minister, Terence O'Neill, and presented a reform package to curb the more obvious excesses of Northern Ireland Unionism. O'Neill turned it down. But when a similar list of reforms was actually worked for and demonstrated for in the Civil Rights campaign of 1968–69, the NIC was nowhere to be found, for by then the reforms had become openly stigmatised as being part of a Catholic plot.

By themselves, Protestant trade-unionists at rank-and-file level behave as trade unionists normally do. They march together in shop-floor contingents; they demonstrate as one. In 1971 one such march took place, led by an engineering shop steward at Belfast shipyards, Billy Hull. The organisation which called the march was the Loyalist Association of Workers. The march was called to demand the immediate introduction of internment. Just a few weeks earlier the same Billy Hull and the same marchers had been involved in another walk-out in protest against the Heath government's Industrial Relations Act. The compatibility of two marches, one protesting against the possibility of jailing, after trial, of trade unionists, the other demanding internment without trial, may appear somewhat obscure; but the greater irony is that the Industrial Relations Act was never even applied to Northern Ireland. What with the low strike-rate, the high profitability, the lack of powerful trade-union leadership and a divided working class, it was not deemed necessary.

7

The Bosses

An Orange song, 'The Orange and the Blue' contains the following two verses:

> Against the altar and the throne
> the democrat may prate,
> But while I am an Orangeman,
> I'll stand for Church and State.
> And I will be an Orangeman
> And brother stand by you,
> While I've a living heart to love
> the Orange and the Blue.
>
> Let not the poor man hate the rich,
> Nor rich on poor look down,
> But each join each true Protestant
> For God and for the Crown,
> And for old England all unite,
> As Orange brethren do,
> Around their 'no surrender' flag,
> The Orange and the Blue.[1]

Almost invariably, those who sing such turgid doggerel, vilifying democrats, acclaiming church and state and venerating love between the poor and rich, are the poor themselves. It is the lower-class Protestants who have little to thank the state for, little reason to be beholden to the rich, who sing the Orange songs with the most gusto and enthusiasm; it is they who have provided the fodder for the Unionist cause. The leaders of Unionism would have been banished to faded oil-canvas long ago had they not been able to rely on such songsters. But they have remained, and while the Protestant lower classes have fought, voted and sung, the Protestant upper classes have led.

That in itself says little about Northern Ireland. What is distinctive about the Orange bosses is not their control, but the manner of their leadership. For example, while it is a truism that the moneyed classes are everywhere wealthy, it is by no means true that they are everywhere prepared to openly finance and promote armed resistance to bourgeois parliaments. Yet this is exactly what Carson, Craig and their friends did in 1913 when they set up that January the Ulster Volunteer Force to resist Home Rule, and followed it in September with a fund to compensate members of the UVF for any loss or disability they might suffer in it. Sir Edward Carson, Sir James Craig, Sir George Clark, Sir James Lonsdale and Lord Dunleath each guaranteed £10,000. Within four months over a million pounds had been subscribed. As the most prominent historian of this period comments: 'In this way the business community of Belfast underwrote the UVF.'[2] It was not only the business community. Unionism in the years of Carson's rebellion included representatives of every wing of the economic establishment. Manufacturers such as Craig, large landowners like Lord Londonderry and Lord Dunleath, lawyers such as Colonel R.H. Wallace, Grand Secretary of the Grand Orange Lodge of Ireland. Even representatives from the British military establishment played their part. Field Marshal Roberts, one of the most prominent British army men, acted as adviser to the Unionists, recommending Sir George Reilly Richardson, commander-in-chief of the UVF (whose previous military career had included campaigns against the Boxer rebellion in China, and in such outposts of the British Empire as Afghanistan, Waziri, Tiri and the Zhod Valley).

The attraction of the Unionist cause to someone like Richardson is understandable, a matter of the white settlers versus the natives so to speak. But such a formula seems an inadequate explanation for the lengths to which the upper classes in Ireland,

and especially the north of Ireland, were prepared to go to defeat Home Rule. What exactly were they protecting in 1913; what exactly were they afraid of in the 1880s; what exactly are they defending in the 1970s? As ever, *The Times* provides a clue to their thinking. In an editorial of May 1913 that newspaper pointed out that Carson's campaign strengthened 'the conservatism of Ulster'. It went on: 'By disciplining the Ulster democracy and by leading it to look up to them as its natural leaders, the clergy and the gentry are providing against the spread of revolutionary doctrine and free thought.'[3]

So much for the notion that the Protestants of Northern Ireland were fighting to preserve freedom of religion.

But strengthening the local ruling class was not the whole story, and the Irish Home Rule supporters could hardly be described as agitators for 'revolutionary doctrine' and 'free thought'. There were further reasons, best explained in the words of the Unionists themselves. Very early on, in the 1880s, the Belfast Chamber of Commerce put their objections to Home Rule in this way:

> This meeting deplores the agitation which now exists for loosening the ties which render Ireland, in all respects an integral part of the United Kingdom and is deeply sensible that all commercial prosperity which has blessed the peaceable parts of this country will receive a sudden shock from any legislation which would have any tendency to imperil the connection between this country and Great Britain.[4]

Despite the popularly held belief that the northerners' interests were somehow different from those of the southern ruling class, the Belfast leaders of industry were not alone in issuing such warnings. At about the same time the Dublin Chamber of Commerce passed an almost identical motion, which read: 'Any measure calculated to weaken the Union . . . would be productive of consequences most disastrous to the trading and commercial interests of both countries.'[5] It was clearly the 'trading and commercial interests' which were to the forefront of the struggle against Irish self-determination. And if this was true for the 1880s, it was also true for the early twentieth century. The Irish Unionist Alliance stated it plainly in a book published in 1907:

> In Ireland the classes that are inevitably opposed to Home Rule . . . include the following; the capitalists, the manufacturers, the merchants, the professional men and indeed all who have anything to lose. The Protestants, with few exceptions, are against it.[6]

There is no denying the accuracy of this statement; it was those who had property to lose, factories and landed estates, who opposed Home Rule; it was Protestants who, with only the smallest of exceptions, were the holders of such fiefdoms. And, as the industrial capital of Ireland was Belfast and the Protestants of Ulster were generally better off than the Catholics both in Ulster and elsewhere, the Ulster Unionists were particularly vociferous in the defence of the status quo. As the Ulster Liberal Unionist Association proclaimed in 1907: 'To a united Ulster which declares, "We will not have disunion, we will not have Home Rule", the future of her prosperity and peace under the sheltering wing of the imperial parliament is assured.'[7] Lord Londonderry, one of the leaders of the Ulster Unionist Party, summed up the position explicitly in 1912:

> Ulstermen believe that the Union with Great Britain has assisted the development of their commerce and industry. The opposition to Home Rule is the revolt of the business and industrial community against the domination of men who have no aptitude for either.
>
> The Ulster Irish League is remarkably lacking in the support of businessmen, merchants, manufacturers, leaders of industry and men who compose a successful and prosperous community.
>
> Ulster's opposition to Home Rule is the hostility of the progressive and advancing people who have made their portion of the country prosperous and decline to hand it over to the control and representatives from the most backward and unprogressive counties.[8]

So Sir George Reilly Richardson's estimation of the cause of Ulster Unionism – the settlers versus the natives – was not a great deal different from the views of the leaders of Ulster Unionism; those who saw themselves as having carved out a prosperous living, as establishing industry, and who now saw their control threatened by the prospect of a democratically controlled Ireland. As a foil to such threats the minority settlers looked to the 'sheltering wing' of the British parliament in which the Irish natives had only a minority voice.

There were times, though, when the Orange establishment's faith in their class brothers in Britain was neither so absolute nor so unconditional. For example, less than fifteen years before the Belfast Chamber of Commerce was pledging loyalty to all things British, the *Belfast News-Letter* proclaimed:

> It is hardly surprising that with the pages of history open before them, with the ruins of their ancient privileges scattered all around, Protestants should care little to maintain a Union which for them henceforth appears to have little value.[9]

The newspaper from whose editorial those words are taken was, and remains, the semi-official voice of the Unionist establishment in Belfast. They are not quoted out of context. They belong merely to a different period, for the Home Rule movement which the editor of the *Belfast News-Letter* was later to organise against in the 1880s was founded at the time of the editorial by men of his persuasion, class and religion.

It was founded by Isaac Butt, a Protestant and a former Conservative who set up the Home Government Association in 1870, and noted in his diary that it contained 'principally Protestants and Conservatives . . . all men of some mark and station.'[10] Tory/Protestant control of the HGA did not last very long. The important point is that it existed at all; that an important section of the Irish establishment was prepared to found a political organisation designed to gain a version of Irish self-determination; and all this barely fifteen years before the same forces were

97

mobilising in opposition to it. But as with Edward Carson's on–off love affair with the German Kaiser (see chapter 3), the contradiction is more apparent than real. Their opposition to Home Rule in the 1880s and 1910s derived from the same fears as did their support for it in the early 1870s – that some alliance of forces would reduce their influence over the affairs of Ireland. In the 1870s the alliance was that between Gladstone and the Liberal Party on the one hand, the Irish Catholic clergy and their adherents on the other. It had achieved a massive vote for the Liberals in the 1868 general election and, in return, the passing of the Irish Disestablishment Act of 1869 and a mild measure of land reform. For the upper-class Protestants the disestablishment of the Anglican church in Ireland was bad enough; technically it was a breach of the Act of Union. More important, the alliance between a major English political party and representatives of the Irish peasantry, even if only their religious representatives, threatened a major shift in the balance of power in Ireland. In short, if Westminster could not be relied upon to look after the interests of the Irish upper classes, of what benefit was Westminster? Of what benefit was the Union if the economic and social order was to be changed?

It was such thinking which produced the phenomenon of a Home Rule movement led by the forces of Unionism. In the 1880s, when the Home Government Association became transformed into a popular movement, the tactic changed and the Irish Tories reverted to the more conventional stance of professing loyalty to the British crown. The means changed, but the ends remained the same – the preservation of the 'ancient privileges' glorified in that editorial from the *Belfast News-Letter*.

So there are a series of myths. There is one which says the Unionists in Northern Ireland, and before them the Unionists in all of Ireland, have no interest, no motivation other than maintaining the constitutional link with Great Britain. There is another legend that Ulster Protestants are fervently loyal to the British crown. The myths have been rebutted again and again by the Unionists themselves. In 1912 Lord Londonderry rejected them because his interests were 'the revolt of the business and industrial community against the domination of men who have no aptitude for either'. Before him spoke Isaac Butt, looking across the Irish Sea at the reforming Liberal government: 'A time may come when every Irishman may wish that we had in Ireland a parliament and a government which an English revolution could not touch.'[11] And in 1972, in the words of the arch-loyalist William Craig's Ulster Vanguard Party:

> Union with Great Britain was never an end in itself for Unionists. It was always a means of preserving Ulster's British tradition. . . . Recent experience suggests that a Westminster administration of Ulster affairs would be representative of the social mores of the larger island and insensitive towards the rather old-fashioned Ulster which progressives despise. In any case British society is already showing signs of instability itself as it is overtaken by the crisis of social and moral values that come upon advanced western societies.[12]

This is the sort of thinking that led William Craig, like the Unionist leaders of 1912 before him, to advocate an independent Ulster, just the sort of thinking that throws into question a final myth, this time one held by primitive 'marxists', that the Northern Ireland ruling class wish to remain in Britain in order to secure free access to the British market. This final myth leaves everything unanswered. It can explain neither the Isaac Butts nor the William Craigs. It ignores the fact that the leadership of the resistance to Irish democracy in the early twentieth century came not from the industrial bourgeoisie alone but also from the landed agricultural classes who would have had access to the British market, with or without Home Rule. Indeed, in 1912 Ulster's economy was still largely based on agriculture and as late as 1926 agriculture in Northern Ireland still employed the largest number of workers.[13] It also ignores the fact that every measure of Home Rule introduced by the Liberals and supported by the major Irish nationalist parties up to 1918 reserved for Westminster the right to legislate on all matters of trade.

The people in control when the Northern Ireland state emerged reflected the interests behind that state. Of the seven ministers in James Craig's cabinet from 1921 to 1937, three were former presidents of the Belfast Chamber of Commerce, one was a partner in a large firm of solicitors, another industrialist and company director, and another the titled owner of one of the largest landed estates in Northern Ireland. The composition of the rest of the Northern Ireland parliament tells the same story. Lawyers and company directors, including a number of the leading linen magnates, made up half of the membership, and a further quarter were from the titled and landed classes.[14]

With such plutocracy in power it is hardly surprising that internal oppositions sprang up of the kind we saw earlier (see chapter 4). Some of them seemed dangerous. In the 1925 Northern Ireland general election the Unionist Party lost eight of their forty parliamentary seats to independent populist Unionist, Labour and tenants' candidates. The need to find a way out was all the more urgent for James Craig because wherever the Unionist establishment had been challenged by candidates who were not nationalists or republicans they had, with only one exception, lost. The threat came from within. Clearly, it fed on the wretched social and economic conditions within Northern Ireland, but what made it effective was the voting system for election to the Northern Ireland parliament; proportional representation based on a transferable vote in multi-member constituencies. Independent candidates had a better chance of being elected under this system because there was no such thing as a wasted vote; if a voter's first preference finished bottom of the poll the vote was transferred to the elector's second preference. This made it impossible for the Unionist Party to argue that a split vote would let in an anti-partition candidate; it meant that a Protestant voter could vote for a non-Unionist without endangering the constitutional position. In the 1925 general election many Protestants did exactly that. Craig reacted crudely and simply: he changed the voting system, replacing proportional representation with single-member constituencies and no transferable vote. As Craig saw it:

> We in Ulster are and ought to be a happy community. Adversity has taught us the value of unity. Unity has brought us our present state of peace and contentment. . . . Mr Devlin and his [Nationalist] party are the natural opposition. Why should any loyalist constituency add strength to it and weaken the influence of my colleagues and myself?[15]

> What I have been afraid of under the proportional representation system was that certain members might be returned to the House who in a crisis upon the one point of vital importance to the Ulster people, might not stand on which side it was intended they should stand when elected. Therefore I will welcome this opportunity to get down to the simple issue, instead of the complicated ones that are inevitably brought before us under the old plan.[16]

The 'simple issue' which Craig referred to was the link with Britain, on which he knew he could achieve majority support. The 'complicated ones' he wished to avoid were housing, unemployment and so on, the issues on which he knew, indeed which the 1925 election had taught him, he and his party were extremely vulnerable. By allowing the electorate only one choice Craig ensured that the Protestant vote would always go to the Unionist Party because any other vote could allow in an anti-partitionist. The tactics paid off handsomely in the 1929 general election. The Unionist Party, campaigning with such slogans as 'Safety First – Vote Unionist'[17] and 'Beware of Independents: Up Ulster: Scatter Your Enemies'[18] regained five of the seats it had lost to pro-partition independents in 1925. Significantly, in the one ward where proportional representation was retained, the Queens University seat, the Unionist Party lost a seat to an independent Unionist.

The 1929 general election was the precursor of many

elections in which the Unionist establishment campaigned on the border issue alone, in which they warned against splitting the loyalist vote and argued that such 'complicated' topics as the wretched economic and social conditions in which the majority of the Northern Ireland population lived, were not at issue. Until the 1969 general election it was to be the Unionist Party's chief tactic; it was a major means by which the Orange upper class maintained control and authority over the Protestant working class. But while the abolition of proportional representation effectively stifled the parliamentary expression of Protestant working-class protest, the protest remained and sought other outlets. None was more ominous for the Unionist Party leadership than that which broke out in the winter of 1932.

It began, ironically enough in the Northern Ireland House of Commons on 30 September, when Tom Henderson attempted to secure an immediate debate on unemployment. After several fiery exchanges, the Speaker ruled the request out of order and then had his mace thrown at him by the solitary Labour MP. His frustration was felt more keenly by the unemployed themselves, and at the beginning of October 1932 workers on an unemployment relief scheme in Belfast went on strike for more working hours and, accordingly, more pay. On 3 October the men held a massive demonstration addressed by nationalist, Labour and independent Unionist speakers. As always the *Belfast News-Letter* was quick to recognise the dangers of such an alliance for the Unionist establishment:

> An admittedly serious state of affairs is being seized upon by socialist and nationalist orators, not so much with discovering some practical remedy as in hope of discrediting the authorities and to paving the way for revolutionary changes, with or without turmoil, in the direction of an experiment in socialism or incorporation of the province in an Irish Republic.[19]

The alarm was echoed by Unionist MP Captain Dixon who, in addition to blaming 'the enemies of Ulster', credited the entire situation to 'people from across the channel',[20] a peculiar bogey for someone tied in kinship with those very people. At first this sort of scaremongering made little impression: when an unemployment demonstration was banned by the government on 5 October, rioting broke out in the heart of Protestant Belfast, in Sandy Row. Police baton-charged the rioters and did so again the following night. The unemployed then announced plans for a rent strike and for a massive demonstration on the 11 October. Again the march was banned by the government, again the marchers attempted to defy the ban, and again the police attacked, although this time the foray was conducted in the Falls Road of Catholic Belfast. Let a journalist at the scene take up the story:

> When Orangemen and Catholics, the lines of starvation already etched on their hollow cheeks, gripped hands and declared emotionally 'Never again will they divide us' there was consternation in the ranks of professional politicians. . . . On the Shankill Road crowds of growling men lounged around waiting. . . . Suddenly a big red-faced woman with a black shawl thrown over her shoulders, wisps of hair hanging from eyes, appeared, almost from nowhere. . . . She ran to crowds of men and in quick terse language told them that the unemployed and the police were in conflict on the Falls Road. 'Are you'se going to let them down?' she almost shrieked. 'No by heavens we are not', they roared back and in almost a twinkling a veritable orgy of destruction began.[21]

Belfast proceeded to suffer what was described in the local press as the worst rioting the city had seen for fifty years, but this time the rioting was strictly non-sectarian. Shots were fired at the police on the Falls Road and in the Shankill trams were seized, barricades were built and the police were attacked with everything that came to hand. By the end of it two people had been shot dead by the police, one in the Shankill, one in the Falls and thirty people had been injured. Of those listed in the *Belfast News-Letter* on 12 October, eleven came from predominantly Protestant areas, nine from Catholic areas, and five from mixed areas.

The government surrendered at once. Unemployment relief

was trebled and the leaders of the unemployed called off the rent strike. But then the Unionist establishment adopted a strategy to avoid ever being faced with such a challenge again. One Unionist politician blamed 'communist Sinn Fein'[22] and James Craig presented the actions of the unemployed as an attack on Northern Ireland's constitutional position: 'To those mischief-makers in our midst I say that if they have any designs that this is a step towards securing an Irish Republic for all of Ireland then I say never'.[23] The Orange Order concentrated its attacks on the evils of communism:

> We desire to impress upon all the loyal subjects of the King, the vital necessity of standing on guard against communism . . . whose aim and object is to overthrow authority, the will of the people and everything we hold sacred in our domestic and public lives.[24]

The Unionist establishment did more than preach and smear, for the large unemployment in Northern Ireland was a boil which was likely to burst again at any moment. It adopted the policy of the Ulster Protestant League; namely that Protestants should employ only Protestants. This was the time Brooke made the statements quoted on p. 40 above, and James Craig was shortly to whip up sectarianism by boasting about his 'Protestant Parliament' and his 'Protestant State'.

The sectarian campaign had its desired effect. In the 1933 election the independent Unionist and Labour vote fell from 38,836 to 33,751 in the six working-class parliamentary constituencies of Protestant Belfast.[25] When, in 1935, Belfast suffered renewed rioting it was completely sectarian. Nine people died, over a hundred were injured and 95 per cent of those worst affected were Catholics. Three hundred Catholic families were driven from their homes and many were driven from their workplaces as the Protestant workers put into practice Basil Brooke's injunction. At the inquest on the victims the city coroner commented:

> Party passion is a very inflammable commodity, bigotry is the curse of peace and goodwill. The poor people who commit these riots are easily led and influenced. . . . They are influenced almost

entirely by the public speeches of men in high and responsible positions. There would be less bigotry if there were less public speech-making by the so-called leaders of public opinion . . . it is not good Protestantism to preach a gospel of hate and enmity towards those who differ from us in religion and politics.[27]

Such is the historical record of the Unionist bosses. And if the 1920s and 1930s seem distant from the 1970s, or if it seems that the leaders of the Unionist establishment have taken to heart the words of the Belfast city coroner of 1935, then let the words of Brian Faulkner stand as a correction. Brian Faulkner, Northern Ireland's last Prime Minister, now projected as the moderate who was defeated by the forces of extremism:

> Two attitudes of mind given great publicity today are more dangerous to our future than the activities of the IRA. The first is that the nationalists, north and south, have had a change of heart about our constitutional position. The second is that the Orange Institution is purely a religious body and must not take part in politics. Let these two fallacies gain ground and our days are numbered. There is a need for a determined and uncompromising attitude.[28]

> When we in the Unionist party defend ourselves against the attacks of the Nationalist Party we are perforce defending ourselves against the Roman Catholic hierarchy.[29]

8

The Fenians

By December 1971 Brian Faulkner and the Unionist Party were tottering on the brink of extinction. Having gambled everything on a policy of internment, Faulkner had seen that policy turn into the greatest military, political and human catastrophe in all the years of Unionist rule in Northern Ireland. Described on his election to the leadership of the Unionist Party as the ablest politician in Northern Ireland, Faulkner had made blunder after blunder and ended up being assailed from the right, the left and even from ruling circles in London. He had adopted a policy of internment because as Minister of Home Affairs he had used the same policy to defeat the 1956–62 IRA 'border campaign'. But he had not noticed that things had changed; he did not understand that the Catholic population of Northern Ireland had, to borrow its favourite cliché, crawled from the gutter and would not easily return. But he had not run out of rhetoric and in a major speech that month he declared:

> We are told that the Northern Ireland majority would have nothing to fear in a united Ireland. We can only judge that proposition on what has happened in the south since the Free State was established. We have seen the Protestant minority there, no matter what is said about fair treatment, steadily diminishing in number and influence. We have seen established in that country a type of society totally alien to the Northern majority. . . . We are asked to throw in our lot with a community whose record in education, house-building and in the development of the social services lags abysmally behind the British performance.[1]

It was an old and effective argument which the Unionist Party had successfully employed for fifty years. But in 1971 it did neither

Faulkner nor his party much good. Not because the Protestants had undergone some magical conversion to the cause of Irish republicanism, but because the Unionist Party which had survived on its ability to beat the Orange drum louder than anyone else was being out-drummed by forces from within its own constituency. In the end, what brought down Brian Faulkner was the belief within the loyalist ranks that he was 'soft' on the question of a united Ireland, too willing to accommodate the major Catholic opposition party, the Social Democratic and Labour Party (SDLP) – too lenient towards the IRA. The battle for the Protestant majority between Faulkner, Craig and Paisley was fought over traditional territory: who was the most steadfast in his opposition to the 'fenians', who was most aware of the threat from the Catholic masses.

The nature of that threat was more imagined than real, but the fear felt of the 'fenians' cannot be simply attributed to a Calvinist paranoia on the part of the Protestant masses or to Unionist misrepresentation of Irish nationalist intentions. In the first place the Protestant lower classes had something to lose (see chapter 2), although that too is not the total explanation. What need to be taken into account are the political alternatives which the 'fenians' offered, and their reasons for proving incapable of attracting substantial Protestant support. For the Protestants have not existed, and never will exist, in a vacuum; however much they like to think otherwise, they have reacted as well as initiated. Indeed modern Unionism was born out of just such a reaction.

The major constant in the fenian world seen by the Protestant lower classes, overshadowing all others like some crippled obesity, is the twenty-six counties: the Irish Free State, Eire, the Irish Republic, or whatever designation that political entity attached to itself after 1921. This is not the place for a detailed analysis of 'the South', as it is called by the Protestants of Northern Ireland. All that needs to be done is to record the failures, because it is those failures that structured the attitude caught in one of the few witty slogans the Protestant community has produced: 'Six into Twenty-six Won't Go'. The reasons for that attitude are not difficult to understand. The twenty-six counties comprise the only state in the western world which show a decline in population this century: from 2,971,823 in 1926 to 2,884,602 in 1966 (compared with an increase in the North from 1,256,561 to 1,484,775, despite a lower birth rate). As table 8.1 shows, the young and productive are more liable to stay where they are in the north than their counterparts in the south.

8.1 Distribution of Population by Age, North and South Ireland, 1961

	0–14 years	15–44 years	over 45 years
	per cent		
Twenty-six counties	42·3	36·4	21·3
Six counties	39·0	39·4	21·6

Data: 1961 census, Northern Ireland; 1961 census, Republic of Ireland

In 1969, when the Civil Rights movement in Northern Ireland was drawing attention to the appalling housing conditions in their state, Dublin alone had 20,000 on a housing list which required that the applicant have at least two children. In the Republic as a whole something like 400,000 people were inadequately housed.[2] At the same time the Republic had the worst house-building record in western Europe: 4·2 per 1,000 people compared with 12·7 in Sweden, 9·0 in Denmark and 7·6 in the UK (in 1967).[3]

Northern Ireland may be a deeply unequal society; but the south is no different. In 1972 5 per cent of the adult population in the Republic owned 72 per cent of the total wealth, or rather more than that, since these figures do not take into account the estates which avoided death duty through the use of family trusts.[4] Conversely,

52 per cent of the total southern Irish labour force earned less than £13 per week in 1965,[5] and the average national wage as a whole in the twenty-six counties has, as with old age pensions, unemployment benefit and the like, been constantly lower than in even the six counties.

From the point of view of the Protestant lower classes these failures justified hostility towards any takeover by the forces of Irish nationalism. In addition, southern society, while hardly deserving the description of 'Rome Rule', harboured a Catholic influence which reached far beyond the chapel gates. It reached into the censorship of literature with the banning of such pagan influences as James Joyce and Edna O'Brien; it reached the cinema screens and made film-going in Ireland, at least until very recently, an exercise in detective-work, so heavily employed were the censor's scissors. (Although as far as film censorship goes the 'good Protestant' is not far removed from the 'good Catholic' as was proven on one of the few occasions Gerry Fitt, now leader of the SDLP, and Eileen Paisley, wife of Ian, voted together on the Belfast corporation to ban the film version of *Ulysses*.) But the point to be made about censorship, as well as about more contentious issues such as the prohibition of birth control, is that in the eyes of the Belfast Protestant the government of the Republic has consistently legislated to apply a mode of social behaviour which goes against the Protestant way of life.

Nor is it simply a question of legislation. If James Craig can be, as he should, accused of maliciousness for his 'Protestant Parliament for a Protestant State', what of these words, spoken by Brendan Corish, now leader of the Irish Labour Party?

> I am an Irishman second, I am a Catholic first. . . . If the hierarchy gives me any direction with regards the Catholic social teaching or Catholic moral teaching I accept without qualification, and in all respects, the teachings of the hierarchy to which I belong.[6]

Or note these sentiments, expressed by a former Irish Prime Minister: 'I have no doubt that all my colleagues . . . would not be a party to any proposals affecting moral questions which would or might come into conflict with the definite teachings of the Catholic church.'[7] One such 'moral question' is that of divorce, and it was precisely on this issue that the Home Ruler Thomas Kettle wrote in 1912, in an effort to persuade Irish Protestants that their fears of a Roman takeover were groundless: 'We Catholics voluntarily abjure the blessings of divorce, but we should never dream of using the civil law to impose our abnegation on those of another belief.'[8] But the heirs of Kettle did more than 'dream'; divorce was specifically banned under the 1937 Irish Constitution, the same constitution which claimed the right of the twenty-six county parliament to 'exercise jurisdiction' over the north. Seeing these two clauses side by side, the antipathy of Protestants is understandable.

It is also understandable that when the young radicals took to the streets of Derry on 5 October 1968 in the Civil Rights march that was to change it all, they should carry banners proclaiming 'Tories Out, North and South', and that when the representative of the Green Tories, Eddie MacAteer, leader of the Nationalist Party, attempted to address the marchers he should be shouted down. That particular confrontation between MacAteer and the young radicals was to be forgotten when the Royal Ulster Constabulary rioted against the marchers and gave the Civil Rights movement its baptism of fire, but it echoed another constant in the relationship between Protestants and the relationship between Protestants and the nationalist cause – the division within that cause between moderates, constitutionalists, Home Rulers or compromisers on the one hand and on the other those who have called themselves, or have been dubbed, republicans, extremists, terrorists or men and women of principle. Those involved have included Charles Parnell and Michael Davitt, Joe Devlin and Jim Larkin, John Redmond and James Connolly; the encounters have been over a whole series of issues, but one in particular – how to win the Protestants to the nationalist cause.

The encounter between Parnell and Davitt dates from the late

1870s and early 1880s, when a mass movement of the Catholic lower classes was threatening to overthrow the existing social set-up in rural Ireland. The conditions which produced this movement were based on a land system which John Stuart Mill described as 'the worst in Europe',[9] in which 75 per cent of those who owned or held agricultural land in Ireland occupied just 12 per cent of the total acreage.[10] In the late 1870s the conditions were worsened by a generalised economic recession which resulted in a large number of evictions. The tenants resisted and in October 1879 the Irish National Land League was established, with Charles Parnell as president and Michael Davitt, a member of the Irish Republican Brotherhood or 'fenians', as the moving force.

The aims of the Land League were a reduction in rents in the short term and, in the long term, the establishment of peasant proprietorships through compulsory state-aided purchase. Davitt himself went further and advocated land nationalisation. The league won immediate support from large sections of the peasantry and was important in mobilising them to resist evictions, attack the property of the landlords and agents and set up their own courts in the Land War which followed. One result was, according to a House of Lords report in September 1881, a partial, and at times complete, breakdown in the normal legal processes.[11]

In the early stages of the Land War the general reaction of Protestant tenants in Ulster was hostile. They tended to be better off than tenants elsewhere (see chapter 2); they were repelled by the presence in the League of avowed nationalists such as Parnell and Davitt; and they knew that the majority of the victims of the League were Protestant, if only because there were vastly more Protestant than Catholic landlords. But within a year of its establishment some Protestant tenants began to move towards the League. In the autumn of 1880 branches had been set up in Donegal, Armagh, Enniskillen and Belfast, and in January 1881 Davitt addressed a meeting in Armagh, chaired by the Grand Master of the Orange Order of the area. The following month Davitt was jailed, but he was later to claim to have had a good deal of success in Ulster and

111

'in fact had I had a few more months I would have brought the whole province into the League'.[12] This may be overstated, but an independent witness of a Land League meeting at Lurgan, County Armagh noted that 'Orangemen joined the League in vast numbers'.[13]

This was exactly the sort of response Davitt was seeking. He was what the British press would today call a 'diehard republican', but like many so described his aspirations were not confined to securing a constitutionally independent Ireland. He was a social radical, and subsequently appeared on Labour and trade-union platforms in England. But although he was the organiser and brains behind the land agitation, Davitt was never in complete control, and especially after he was jailed the reins of power were gathered up increasingly by Parnell. Parnell was no social radical, and although he supported the Land League he did so to maintain his own position as a nationalist leader and jettisoned the agitation once he could safely do so. As soon as the Second Land Act was passed, giving the tenants an independent rent assessment, fixity of tenure and the right to profit from any improvements they made, Parnell called off the Land War, disbanded the League and replaced it with the National League, which he chiefly employed to organise his parliamentary party. He encouraged the Catholic clergy to participate in the National League as a counterweight to the radicals, with the result that at the county conventions which in theory selected the parliamentary candidates the average attendance comprised 150 laymen and 50 clergy.[14]

For Michael Davitt the change in the direction of the movement was disastrous. He described the formation and the operation of the National League as 'The complete eclipse by a purely parliamentary substitute of what had been a semi-revolutionary organisation. It was in a sense the overthrow of a movement, the enthronement of a man, the replacing of nationalism by Parnellism.'[15] The impact on the Protestants of Ulster can easily be imagined. Some at least had begun to support a movement they had at first seen as little more than a Papist plot.

And then that movement changed its nature, its policy of radical land reform, albeit with republican overtones, being replaced by a policy confined to Home Rule; to all appearances, it became heavily influenced by the Catholic church.

These two contrasting approaches within the Irish national movement – the one content to gain some form of constitutional independence however limited, the other aimed at a much grander design of political, social and economic independence, seeking the mobilisation of all the toilers of Ireland – did not end with Parnell and Davitt. They re-emerged at the turn of the century in the conflict between John Redmond and Joe Devlin on the one hand and Larkin and Connolly on the other, and never more clearly than during the 1907 Belfast strike (see chapters 5 and 6).

Devlin's role in the strike has a particular significance. It was not until the strike had been in progress for a month that he made his views known at a public meeting addressed by Larkin, Tom Sloan and a leading Protestant trade unionist, Alexander Boyd. Devlin explained that he had not come out openly in support of the strike until that moment because he feared the Unionist press would whip up sectarianism if he did. At the time the strike was solid and appeared to have every chance of success, but two months later when it had gained only a very limited victory, Devlin told a different story:

> Let me say that I knew nothing about the strike in its progress and I do not think I even know to the present moment what the absolute results of the strike were . . . I have never spoken to Mr Larkin in my life, but once . . . I have never received communication from either Mr Larkin or anyone connected with the strike during its progress, before it commenced or after it ended.[16]

Devlin took a similar stand in 1913 when his Ancient Order of Hibernians (modelled as an exclusively Catholic equivalent to the Orange Order) and the Nationalist Party denounced Larkin during the great Dublin Lock-Out. In fact the history of the AOH during Devlin's presidency was one of anti-trade unionism to the extent, on occasion, of setting up scab unions.[17]

This attitude to the labour movement was not the only difference between the Redmond/Devlin and the Larkin/Connolly wings of the Irish national movement. Devlin and Redmond both supported the British war effort in 1914–18, while Connolly was one of the few socialists in Europe to label the war imperialist and to refuse to take sides. Devlin approved the Liberal proposals in 1914 to exclude Ulster from the jurisdiction of a Home Rule parliament for a period, while for Connolly implementing them would 'Make the unity of the Irish nation a subject to be decided by the votes of the most bigoted and passion-blinded reactionaries in those four counties where such reactionaries are in a majority.'[18]

The Parnells, Redmonds and Devlins differed from the Davitts, Larkins and Connollys on more than the labour question, the national question or the war question. Connolly's vision of Ireland – a republican, workers', socialist Ireland – made him (and Larkin and Davitt) try to reach the Protestant workers, but without compromising with the forces of Orange reaction. Devlin's vision (and Redmond and Parnell's) – a sectarian Catholic, capitalist and pro-imperialist Ireland – precluded such tactics. They had nothing to offer the Protestant working class so they either ignored it or compromised with its political masters. Thus, after the Northern Ireland state was established in 1921 Devlin's Nationalist Party mirrored Craig's Unionist Party – the Catholic party for the Catholic people.

The ideas held by Devlin/Redmond and Connolly/Larkin did not die with them; they have emerged with renewed vigour in the current struggle. When the Civil Rights marchers shouted down Eddie MacAteer on the 5 October 1968, they were attacking the heir to Devlin's Nationalist Party. The manner of that march was also an affront to that party. By wanting to take their march through the Protestant areas of Derry they were implying, first of all, that their demands were in no sense offensive to Protestants; but, equally important, they were rejecting the electoral policies of the Nationalist Party, which rarely put forward candidates in

Protestant areas. The marchers of 5 October carried placards proclaiming 'Class Not Creed'. They rejected the view that their ideas should be confined to the Catholic ghettos.

People's Democracy, the Belfast grouping which emerged out of the events of 5 October, fought the 1969 Stormont election in both Catholic and Protestant constituencies. Bernadette Devlin, standing as an independent in a Westminster by-election, canvassed strongly in Protestant areas, even though the Catholic vote in her constituency was enough to have achieved her election. Eamonn McCann, the main organiser of 5 October, stood as a Labour candidate in the 1969 Stormont election and held meetings in Protestant areas where previously a non-Unionist politician had never dared to step. As it turned out, little came of it. The concentration on the social and economic issues at the expense of the national question flew in the face of Northern Ireland reality. In the final analysis, the issue was not how many reforms could be won from the Orange state – there were not many anyway – but the very existence of that state.

The leaders of People's Democracy, together with Bernadette Devlin and Eamonn McCann, were to realise their mistakes with the same kind of hindsight that is embodied here.[19] They were confused about their strategy; they failed to take the opportunities that arose after 5 October; most of all they failed to build a socialist organisation. But, however short they fell of what was necessary, it was nothing compared to what was committed by the heirs of Joe Devlin.

There is little point in recording the history of these people, the John Humes and Ivan Coopers, in the last few years. The very fact that they are called 'moderates' by a British press which also calls the British army 'peacekeepers' is indication enough of who they are and where they stand. As for their approach to the Protestant working class they have had as little to offer as had Joe Devlin. They made it clear throughout the early days of the Civil Rights movement that they wanted no more than to divide more equally the crumbs allowed to the workers by the Orange bosses. John Hume in 1969:

> All that requires to be done is to grant the remaining demands of the civil rights movement – democratic representation in local government and an end to the Special Powers Act. . . . It would be a shame if all the major injustices were not removed now.[20]

But for many the major injustices were not the unfair voting system or even the draconian Special Powers Act; they were the unemployment, the poverty, the homeless, and indeed the very existence of the Orange state. The reaction of the Protestant working class to such statements hardly needs telling. If John Hume wanted no more than to take away their marginal privileges, then who can wonder that they refused to listen?

The leaders of what was to become the Social Democratic and Labour Party also shared with Joe Devlin his Catholic exclusiveness. In the June 1970 election Eamonn McCann stood against Eddie MacAteer. Hume, who had fought MacAteer (and McCann) in a three-cornered contest for the Foyle constituency the previous year as a Civil Rights candidate and had won, now came out in support for MacAteer and accused McCann of splitting the Catholic vote. Is it any wonder that the Protestants concluded that the Civil Rights movement was nothing other than a Papist plot?

What of the others, some who claimed to be different, even claimed to be the heirs of Connolly? The most notable is the Official Republican movement, which announces its class politics with every James Connolly badge it sells, yet has beaten the Catholic drum as loudly as Joe Devlin:

> The Civil Rights movement is a united front of people who agree on the basic Civil Rights programme, however much they might disagree on other things. Republicans, Labour men, socialists, liberals, nationalists and even some Unionists have given their support. In particular it has united all the Catholic people because the Catholics are discriminated against as *Catholics* in Northern Ireland . . . all the more mistaken therefore are the enthusiastic but inexperienced people of the People's Democracy who think they can help things by turning the Civil Rights programme into a

116

socialist one . . . the Civil Rights movement cannot afford disunity of this kind, however disguised it may be with radical phrases and 'revolutionary' sounding worlds. [their original emphasis][21]

In mid-1969 the Official-controlled Civil Rights Association refused to condemn the Republican government's sectarian policies on divorce and contraception and so barred the door to the few Protestant sympathisers who really did judge the civil rights issue to be 'non-political'.

The parallels between the Officials and Joe Devlin are strong and became more evident as the political crisis of Unionism developed. Just as Devlin had been willing to accept partition, and with it the Orange state, so in the 1970s the Officials' sole demands were for a Bill of Rights, and a 'democratic' Stormont. And, as the vision of Catholic unity peacefully petitioning for justice became increasingly vulnerable after 1969, their attempts to compromise with Orangeism took on new and increasingly bizarre forms. They started talking with the Protestant paramilitaries, to open a bridge to the Protestant working class, but on the Protestants' terms; and since the question of republican Ireland was not negotiable for the Protestants, it was not raised. They talked, instead, about campaigning against new motorways. They took a more sinister turn when, in the summer of 1975, their paper published an article from the UVF, calling for the physical elimination of members of the Irish Republican Socialist Party who had split from the Officials' reformism.

After 1968 the Officials moved plumb into the centre of the Parnell/Redmond/Devlin tradition – Catholic unity, avoidance of the national issue and, finally, total compromise with Orangeism. This was not a prescription to appeal to the radical wing of Protestantism.

The other wing of the Republican movement, the Provisionals, fit the category of neither Devlin nor Connolly, and will be treated later. Let it just be said here that to call Protestant workers 'deluded Irishmen' is, to say the least, simplistic.

There have been those, from the earliest days of the nationalist movement, who have approached the Protestant working class honestly and seriously. That they have little to show for their efforts may be due in part to their own failings, but at least they have tried, without compromising with Orangeism, to chart a path to their fellow-workers. As for the others, the political leaders of the 'fenians' who have climbed to the top by relying on Catholic unity and Catholic power, by kowtowing to British imperialism – let them recognise that the monster of the Protestant working class, if monster it be, has been created out of many elements: out of prejudice and privilege created by the British and sustained by the Orange bosses, but also reinforced by the cosy, self-satisfied narrow-minded men who have governed the twenty-six counties and by their counterparts in the North who have always sought the easy option.

9

Protestantism's Last Stand

In the early hours of Sunday, 26 June 1966, four Catholics were shot leaving the Malvern Arms public house in the Shankill district of Belfast. One of the four, Peter Ward, was killed – because he was a Catholic and because he was in the company of a man suspected of being in the then largely defunct IRA. Northern Ireland in 1966 was a relatively peaceful place, free of open sectarian violence; there seemed no sane reason for the shootings. The man later convicted for being in charge of the murder gang was Augustus Spence, leader of the Ulster Volunteer Force. Spence was universally condemned at the time, not only by church leaders, politicians and the like but also by Spence's own working-class community. He killed for no reason and there were few who complained when he was sentenced to life imprisonment.

Five years later Spence had become a folk hero in the Protestant working-class community and 'Gusty' joined all the other slogans on the walls of Protestant Belfast. Gusty had foreseen it all and tried to prevent the uprising before it had a chance to start. What happened in Northern Ireland after 1968 converted Gusty Spence from a murderer to a freedom fighter. Gusty Spence wrote poems in prison, some of which were later printed in the loyalist newspapers of the early 1970s. One of these poems follows:

An Extremist

An extremist is a person who holds his
    faith extremely,
This point of view to timid folk might appear
    unseemly,

But timid folk did not come forth when Extremists
    did enjoin,
To fight alongside William at the Battle of
    the Boyne.

In the Ulster crisis an arch Extremist, Sir Edward,
    took the reins,
And the Covenant was signed in blood from
    many an Extremist's veins,
Fronted by an Empire they defiantly stood
    their ground,
Whilst as usual the timid folk were in hiding
    to be found.

The same Extremists bled and died for Ulster
    thru the ages,
Many famous names are written down in
    history's time-worn pages,
They gave their all while timid folk, being
    timid folk, stay home,
And lived in dread of the hells declared for
    those that serve not Rome.

So when Ulster is in danger the Extremist will
    take a hand,
Because they have an extreme love towards their
    native land,
A faith, a Crown and a way of life they will
    never sacrifice,
But fight like loyal Ulstermen and not timid
    ULSTER MICE.[1]

Gusty was right. It was not he who broke with tradition. 'Scatter Your Enemies', Unionism had said in the 1920s and 1930s.[2] The Protestant poor could not be expected to appreciate that times, interests and tactics had changed for the leaders of the Unionist alliance.

The history of Northern Ireland since the 1960s is the history of these changes. They have been documented, described and analysed more than anything else in Irish history, and it is not the intention of this narrative to go over the same ground. But what is long overdue is an account of the Protestant lower class's view of the last eight years, not because of some abstract allegiance to objectivity, but because the determining factor throughout Northern Ireland's latest political crisis has been the way the ordinary Protestant has thought and reacted. It is, for example, the Protestant 'extremists' who, by attacking the Catholic areas of Belfast in August 1969, gave birth to the Provisionals. And the attacks themselves were a reaction by the working-class Protestants of Belfast to the Unionist leadership's refusal to put down the papists in the manner they had done in the past. As with August 1969, so too with every other major turning-point in Northern Ireland's recent history: it has been the developments within the Protestant community that have dictated events.

The first such turning-point was Terence O'Neill's fall from power. The February 1969 election had shown that he no longer enjoyed the confidence of the Protestant lower classes and he was replaced by James Chichester-Clark. That brought no immediate cure and the crisis reached a new high with the Apprentice Boys' March in Derry in August 1969. The march took place against the advice of Sir Arthur Young, sent over from London to control the RUC, and against the advice of Sir Ronald Burroughs, Westminster's representative in Northern Ireland.[3] But since Clark could not afford to further alienate Protestant opinion by banning the march, it took place. The violence that followed led to the introduction of British troops on the 14 August; the determination of the Protestants to march had produced a new deterioration.

The events of August 1969 triggered off a series of British-dictated 'reforms', one of which – the disbandment of the B Specials – hurt the Protestant community badly. It led directly to the first shots being fired at the British army, by Protestants on the Shankill Road. The Protestants continued to make the pace when in March

1971, they forced out Clark for not coming up with a few thousand more British troops to deal with the increasing campaign of the Provisionals. The extra troops would not have changed much, but Clark needed the gesture to fend off the growing political attack from Protestant lower classes; he needed to display the desire for firm measures. In August 1971 Faulkner introduced internment, partly because he trusted such a policy, but also because he needed to appease Protestant critics. Internment brought a massive increase in the Provisionals' campaign and, in consequence, a rise in the pressure which had already ousted O'Neill and Clark. The next great turning-point, in January 1972, was Bloody Sunday, which took place after Paisley had threatened to stop the demonstration if Faulkner did not. Bloody Sunday was Unionism's greatest political disaster yet, and led directly to the suspension of Stormont six weeks later. Direct rule settled little. A new legislative Assembly was established, it failed to secure the old Protestant unity and Faulkner was forced into coalition with the Catholic SDLP. Once more the Protestants reacted – a General Strike brought down the Assembly.

In all these cases it was the alienation of lower-class Protestants from the Unionist leadership which had determined events. It was they who demanded that O'Neill go, that Chichester-Clark act, that internment be introduced, that the Bloody Sunday march be stopped, that security remain in Protestant hands. The attempt of the Unionist Party to secure Protestant unity produced a chronic state of instability within their camp which led to politically suicidal acts by the Protestant mass. Just as they secured their own ascendancy, the Protestants determined their own collapse, as Gusty Spence and the 'timid folk' went their separate ways.

The first hint of separation came in 1965, when the two Irish Prime Ministers, O'Neill and Lemass, met officially for the first time since Partition. Ian Paisley described it prematurely but accurately: 'The policy of the Unionist Party was reversed and the Protestant people's faith in O'Neill was shattered forever.'[4] O'Neill was running a risk when he met Lemass, for reasons that became clear later that year when the Republic excluded Northern Ireland from the operation of its import levy. It had become good business to talk with the dreaded southerners. Even before the talks, the Republic was beginning to change in a direction of some interest to northern businessmen. In 1964 the Manufacturers' Act put paid to the dream of an independent capitalist Ireland, with the dropping of the stipulation, in force since 1938, that 51 per cent of any Irish firm had to be owned by native Irish. In July 1966 the Anglo-Irish Free Trade Agreement came into force and began a ten-year process of phasing out all measures to protect Irish industry and of re-integrating the Irish economy into that of Britain.

It was not Ulster Unionism which surrendered in the O'Neill – Lemass talks, it was Irish republicanism. Not only was the Republic re-integrated with Britain economically, but by agreeing to talk with the Northern Ireland government Lemass give it a de facto recognition, despite the formal claim to sovereignty over the six counties.

Changes within the Northern Ireland economy were working towards the same result. The traditional industries of shipbuilding and linen were in decline and the new large British or multinational companies like ICI and Dupont were neither part of the traditional Unionist structure nor interested in sustaining an anti-Catholic policy in the north which would act as a hindrance to exploiting the developing possibilities of exploitation in the south. The north needed to be 'rationalised'.

Good business sense all this, but it reckoned without the Protestant lower class. From the start of the 'troubles' their reaction was one of confusion, even bewilderment, and certainly frustration. 'Must the Protestants give up everything in the useless quest for appeasement?'[5] ran a letter to the *Belfast Telegraph* in 1971, and that was a general reaction throughout. After the violence of 5 October 1968, when the television cameras recorded the full extent of police brutality, the closed world of the ordinary Protestant had room only for indignation at the accusations against their police and at the general sympathy for the Catholic cause. As a letter to the *Belfast News-Letter* put it: 'Please inform the public that there was no police brutality in Londonderry. Anything meted out was well deserved and those who marched were deliberately seeking trouble.'[6] There was no police violence; if there was any it was well deserved, and, as the marchers were seeking trouble in the first place it was their opponents – the Protestants – who had the right to feel resentful. This was only reasonable:

> I am an employer and I have never asked about the religion of my employees, but I must add that if this agitation continues I will be forced to discriminate.
>
> Signed,
> 'Reasonable'[7]

And, after all,

> The people of Ulster want to live in peace side by side with other religious denominations provided they are not anti-Ulster or anti-British.[8]

For 'people', read Protestants.

The general tone of letters to the press hardened as the troubles intensified. The reforms were seen as concessions, the compromises as appeasement. And yet the restless natives kept crying out for more. In the week before the introduction of internment the columns of the newspapers were filled with demands for action, with protests against the weakness of the government. A letter to the *Belfast Telegraph*:

> A lot of concessions have been granted to the minority by the Stormont government and there are now equal rights for everyone regardless of class or creed. We say intern all IRA members, re-arm the RUC and bring back the B Specials.[9]

But, even after internment:

> It was entirely predictable that the introduction of internment would be followed by a widespread rebel uprising. A resolute Unionist government predicting these attacks would have organised protection for local areas using ex-B Specials and other

loyalists. However at the crucial hour Ulster lacked such a resolute government. . . . And so the Northern Ireland government has once again blundered.[10]

Nothing the Unionist leadership did from October 1968 onwards could please the Protestant 'hardliners' as they came to be known; even internment was considered insufficient.

The great anger came with the suspension of Stormont in March 1972. For three and a half years the Protestants had seen themselves patient and forgiving, granting concession after concession, only to be met by further demands and violence. That this patience was eventually rewarded by the abolition of their own parliament was inexplicable. Two more letters:

> The decision by the British government to suspend Stormont must surely rank with some of the most infamous acts of history.[11]

> There is a heavy stench of treason in the air. Ulster has been betrayed and Stormont executed by the greatest liars the world has ever seen . . . the sell-out to the hobgoblins of the IRA has been completed.[12]

It is pointless explaining to the writers of such letters that the event which finally led to the suspension of Stormont was Bloody Sunday or that 'military solutions' only strengthened the Provisional IRA and put 'Ulster' in yet greater danger. The traditional loyalists invariably reacted within the traditional terms of reference. They saw, as a letter in 1973 put it, that

> This is not the Unionism my forefathers fought for . . . we are all so tired of the weak-kneed Unionism which is now becoming all too common.[13]

They signed their letters 'Frustrated', 'Bewildered', 'Disgusted' in profusion. They could not understand what it was all about, where it would all end, what they had done to deserve it. The closed world, the narrow view through Orange blinkers, determined everything.

In 1972 the *Belfast Telegraph* held an opinion poll in which readers were invited to name their 'man for the hour', 'the

Ulsterman who might unite the community and lead it to peace'. Jesus Christ received a number of votes but the man who topped the poll was Ian Paisley. Never in a thousand Orange marches would any objective observer of Northern Ireland imagine Paisley capable of uniting Protestant and Catholic, but the correspondents to the *Belfast Telegraph* did not see it that way:

> The man for the hour is the Rev. Dr Paisley, MP. As such a leader he has got honesty, integrity and sincerity. He is also a consecrated and sincere man of God. He has the respect and confidence of many Roman Catholics, as well as Protestants. I feel assured he has been called from God for this service.[14]

> I think Dr Ian Paisley is the right man to save Ulster from civil war. He is a straightforward man and always comes to the point. I think he is the reincarnation of St Patrick who is believed to have banished the snakes out of Ireland. It appears however that a few got away and God has chosen Dr Paisley to finish the job. There are many Roman Catholics who were opposed to Dr Paisley earlier on but now have changed their minds because they have discovered that Dr Paisley is a God-fearing man and a Christian gentleman.[15]

Letter-writing was one way the Protestants could work out their frustration, but apart from personal therapy it did not do much good. There were however other ways of protesting, as a final letter, written just after the suspension of Stormont, pointed out:

> People who have suffered so much from the bomber and the murderer now find that the British government has abdicated to the demands of the anarchists. The people who resorted to barbaric tactics have been generously treated with practically all their demands met and the proposals of the peaceful law-abiding majority have not been accepted. By the British government actions it has [been] proved that violence pays and the majority are now being driven to take up the tactics of the minority as the only way forward.[16]

Advocating that Protestants take up the 'tactics of the minority' was all very well, but what did this mean in practice? The traditional means for putting down the natives had either been

126

taken away, as the B Specials were, or had failed, as internment had. The means by which the Protestants had secured their social and economic superiority was supposedly being reformed; the state itself was under threat of extinction. So what was left for the Protestant community to do? The 'tactics of the minority' presumably meant physical violence like that of the Provisionals. But against whom? The Provisionals could shoot British soldiers and the RUC because they regarded them as agents of repression. They could blow up economic targets because it was in line with the general aim of destroying the Ulster state. But the Protestants could do neither – the police and troops were their police and troops, Ulster was their state. The only recognisable enemy were the fenians, the Catholic minority, and although the occasional policeman or soldier was shot by Protestant militants, it was against the Catholic minority that the violence was directed. There was never any great element of sectarianism in the Provisionals' campaign, but the Protestant violence was wholly sectarian. Gusty Spence was vindicated.

Protestant violence was a feature of the troubles from 1968 onwards. Its earliest manifestation was the attack on the peaceful People's Democracy marchers in January 1969 at Burntollet Bridge. Other similar attacks were to follow. They became more deadly in August 1969 when Protestant mobs, including members of the RUC and B Specials, invaded Catholic areas of Belfast, killing six and burning down many homes. But the most cold-blooded campaign came with the suspension of Stormont, when the 'motiveless murders', for the most part of Catholics by Protestants,[17] began in earnest. The Protestant ascendancy may have been collapsing on every front, but at the level of sectarian assassination the loyalist 'extremists' reasserted their superiority with a vengeance. Catholics were killed because they were Catholic; Protestants who were friendly with Catholics were killed because of their friendships. Often the assassinations came only at the end of a long process of brutality and torture. The Provisionals saw themselves as soldiers, they genuinely did defend their

127

community. Not so the Protestant gun-carriers. They set up protection rackets inside their own community; intimidated, even killed, those who refused to contribute. While the differences among the militant Catholics – the Provisionals, the Officials and later the Irish Republican Socialist Party – were essentially political, the differences between the Protestant militants were largely, although not always, concerned with the degree of sectarianism required. Republicans argued whether it was tactically correct to shoot British soldiers or blow up 'economic' targets; loyalists argued whether it was tactically correct to bomb Catholic pubs.

The differences were reflected in the newspapers of the two camps. The republican newspapers contained political analysis and argument; the loyalist papers, when not filled with anti-Catholic jokes and songs, offered obscure threats and cryptic reports concerning anyone suspected of offending the loyalist code. The largest-selling loyalist community newspaper, *Loyalist News*, was particularly prominent in this respect:

> IS IT TRUE – That a so-called Scottish Prod prefers to employ Leeson St layabouts in his cleaning business?

> ANTRIM – It has been pointed out that the 'Jet Set' did not play the 'Queen' in the Stepple Inn last Friday night.[18]

> BALLYCLARE – Is it true that in the Red Hand Bar a collection in aid for the sixteen detained Loyalists was refused?[19]

The effect of such intelligence could be deadly, literally. In September 1972 *Loyalist News* asked its readers: 'What prominent member of the SDLP is keeping company with a Protestant female from Belfast's Crumlin Rd?[20] The two in question were SDLP Assembly member Paddy Wilson and Irene Andrews. The following June both were found stabbed to death.

The different mentalities of the Catholic and Protestant militants were not due to the fact that Catholics were somehow 'nicer' people, but because the different politics of the two communities produced different practices; one community was fighting to maintain a system of privilege, the other was fighting to overthrow it. Accordingly, when the restless natives rose up there was nothing for it but to put them down, and since all Catholics had been discriminated against as Catholics, when the violence began they were shot whether they were members of the IRA or not. Similarly, when organisations such as the Ulster Defence Association found they were recruiting and training men with no noble line of action to propose, men who quarrelled, shot each other and subjected their community to protection rackets, there was little they could do about it. There were no legitimate targets. They could not attack authority because they were, or saw themselves as, the authorities. So they hit out blindly at whomever and whatever they could.

The actions of the Protestant militants did them little good politically and did their cause a great deal of harm. They confirmed the opinion the world had of them as a brutal and uncharitable people; they widened the gulf between themselves and their former partners in the Unionist alliance, the Unionist upper class and the British government. Occasionally, they drove their overlords, the Unionist or British government, against them, a result which brought on even more confusion, bewilderment and anger. Such betrayals were so foreign to their tradition, they were bound to be recorded:

> Red is the colour of the para's hat,
> If you want to wear one you've got to be a rat,
> So watch your step or you'll get shot,
> For paras, paras, are all rats.

> We bought them drinks, we made them tea,
> They seemed like friends to you and me,
> But their smiles were false, their promises hollow,
> When the paras move in then death will follow.

> They murdered two that night in September,

A night that Shankill will always remember,
They died in silence (not a shout)
Killed by a trigger-happy lout.[21]

1968–74 will be remembered by Northern Irish Catholics as the years of the risen people, of a struggle for freedom. They will be remembered by the British as just another example of the intractability of the 'Irish problem'. No historian will remember them as the years of the sell-out of the Protestants because the 'facts' – the denial of civil rights to Catholics, internment operated overwhelmingly against Catholics – do not argue that way. What the facts do argue is that whatever concessions there were, were made to the Protestant militants; that whatever the paper reforms given to the Catholics, the Protestants were given dead Catholics, interned Catholics, the saturation by troops of Catholic areas.

But the Protestants of Northern Ireland do not and will not acknowledge such an interpretation. With one exception, it was a period of defeat, appeasement, surrender. The exception was the UWC strike of March 1974, when they found a weapon that helped them achieve both the solidarity and the victory they had been seeking for six years. A year later the Ulster Workers' Council summed up the strike as

> a historic milestone for the Ulster people. The contrived unrepresentative Executive collapsed. A victory had been gained – not by the UWC or any single loyalist organisation or politician but by the overwhelming majority of a community which had only demanded what was theirs by right. May 1974 gave a hint of the majority population potential in determining their country's future.
>
> Has the lesson been learned by those who think otherwise?[22]

Just who exactly the last sentence was aimed at is obscure. Was it aimed at the British government which, at the time it was written, was still insisting on some form of Protestant–Catholic power-sharing? Was it aimed at those in the Unionist camp, such as Brian Faulkner and the Alliance Party who continued to urge compromise? Was it aimed at those in the Protestant camp who, in May 1975, were still carrying out sectarian assassination – indeed at a greater rate than ever before? Or at the UDA, the UVF, the Ulster Freedom Fighters, the Red Hand Commandos, the Ulster Citizens' Army, the Ulster Volunteer Service Corps, Tara, Protestant Action or any of the many other competing Protestant paramilitary organisations? Or was it aimed at the Democratic Unionist Party, the Vanguard Party, the Ulster Unionist Council or any of the other political organisations in the still divided loyalist camp? Could it have been aimed at Bill Craig, who in September 1975 declared he was ready to consider some form of power-sharing with the SDLP, or Ian Paisley who denounced Craig? Whatever the answer, the facts – that the Protestants were as divided as ever, one year after the victorious strike; that once-hailed leaders such as Craig were again urging compromise; that the paramilitaries were still fighting amongst themselves; that the dominant expression of the Protestant militants' politics was still sectarian assassination – the facts suggest that the 'lesson' the sentence refers to, rather than being learned and taken to heart, had on the contrary proved to be unteachable.

10

'O God our help in ages past,
Our hope for years to come'

The Orange Order's official magazine for the 12 July celebrations in 1975 included a quiz for the weary marchers. Among the twenty-five questions were:

Do You Know

The Williamite General, aged 80, killed at the Battle of the Boyne?

The only Englishman to become Pope?

What football ground in Belfast is named Solitude?

The only man to have been Solicitor General for England and Ireland?

A book of the Bible which does not contain the word God?

How many arches span the Queen Elizabeth and Queen's bridges?

The name of Jacob's daughter?

The only Belfast senior cricket club to originate in a public park?

Where are the tombs of Lord Carson and Lord Craigavon?

A member of the Royal family who was Grand Master of the Orange Order?

When Belfast transport changed from horse to electric tram?

Who replaced Judas Iscariot as apostle?

A Lord Mayor of Belfast who was a member of the Jewish community?[1]

Presumably the quiz was designed to include the sort of information the average Orange marcher would, or should, know. The religious questions were attuned to the scriptural studiousness of the good Protestant; the questions on English and Irish history displayed the links between the two islands; and the question on the resting-places of Carson and Craigavon reminded the Orange marcher of the glorious heroes of old. The questions on sport suggested that the honest Protestant had healthy outdoor interests, and the ones on the geography of Belfast that he was civic-minded. There was even a question on the dreaded Catholic church – know thy enemy? – and the one on the Jewish Lord Mayor of Belfast provided a ready answer to any ignorant critic who imagined Unionism's ruling circle was confined to Protestants. Clearly the upstanding Orangeman was expected to be aware of his political traditions, his religious faith, his town, his sport and to be able to prove the Orange political machine to be non-sectarian.

This peculiar mixture of knowledge and interests has led to quandaries in the past. In 1958 a major political row took place over whether Northern Ireland's football team should compete in the finals of the World Cup, because it would mean playing on Sundays. Football won that particular controversy in a singular triumph of reason. A few years later there were moves to open playing parks on Sundays. Indignation swept the land; politicians, church leaders and civic notables chained themselves to park gates to prevent them opening. Among them was David Bleakley, NILP member and later Minister of Community Relations in Faulkner's government, who notched up one of his rare political victories when the parks stayed closed. Popeheads, of course, play their sports on Sunday, but their souls are lost anyway. After all, it is well known whose side God is on in Northern Ireland, for the booklet printed to celebrate the 1975 'Twelfth' contains a hymn which has become a loyalist anthem in recent years and is sung at all their political rallies:

> O God our help in ages past,
> Our hope for years to come,
> Our shelter from the stormy blast,
> And our eternal home.

Now it is true that God is '*our*' help, '*our*' hope, but it must also be admitted that the stormy blast has rather increased in turbulence in recent years. Even the Almighty, looking down with the special grace He does on the jewel of Ulster, must have had moments of confusion of late. Had He looked at the election to the Ulster Assembly in 1973 He might have encountered difficulty in deciding just who was representing His Chosen People. Alliance? Democratic Unionist? Independent Loyalist? National Front Loyalist? Northern Ireland Labour Party? Independent Pro-White Paper? Loyalist? Official Unionist? Unionist? Unionist Anti-White Paper? Ulster Constitutional Loyalist? Independent Unionist? Vanguard Unionist? In that election there were 166 pro-Unionist candidates contesting 72 seats, 19 of which were won by anti-Unionists; so in effect there were over three Unionist candidates for every available seat.

It seems a long time since Unionist unity could be obtained by simply beating the Orange drum, wearing an Orange sash and calling for a closing of the ranks. Since 1968, instead of healing the splits within Unionism – as had been the case for the previous hundred years – the external threat, first the Civil Rights movement, then the Provisionals, has deepened and widened internal divisions. And the splits themselves, instead of being to the left as hitherto, have since 1968 been towards the right, towards strengthening sectarianism.

There has been one notable exception, the Alliance Party, and it merits discussion not simply because it broke from Unionism to the left but because it tested in practice the viability of attracting widespread Protestant support for a Unionism without sectarianism.

Alliance grew out of the New Ulster Movement, formed to rally support for O'Neill at the time of the leadership crisis in late 1968. The NUM was part of a massive and well-orchestrated campaign. The most widely read Northern Ireland newspaper, the *Belfast Telegraph* printed 'I'm Backing O'Neill' coupons which the public were urged to cut out and send in. The *Telegraph* was joined by the entire Northern Irish, Southern Irish and British news and opinion media in representing O'Neill as the brave moderate man

134

willing to risk his own future in the cause of community harmony, and politicians such as Paisley and Craig as being supported by no more than a few cranks. It was a real shock when Paisley came within a thousand votes of defeating O'Neill in the February 1969 election.

The NUM evolved into Alliance to carry the banner of O'Neillism when the great man himself was dispatched to the House of Lords. Its first conference attracted over a thousand delegates and in a wave of enthusiasm a well-financed and organised party machine was set up. It was the most impressive splinter group Unionism had ever produced. There were two joint chairmen, one a Catholic and the other Bob Cooper, a Protestant and former leading figure in the Young Unionist Association. At first the party attracted O'Neill Unionists and a scattering of Liberal Party and Northern Ireland Labour Party members. It gained its most significant recruits early in 1972 when three Stormont MPs, two Unionists and one Nationalist, went over to it, showing for all to see that all men of good sense could unite under its banner. By the time the election to the new Assembly came in 1973, much was expected of Alliance, not only inside Northern Ireland, but also by the British government, whose main aim was to swell the middle ground which Alliance and its well-mannered, articulate supporters believed to exist. In the Assembly election manifesto Alliance described itself, not immodestly, as 'the First Sign of Hope' and urged the voters to 'Vote for New People with New Politics'; to 'grasp this historic opportunity to unite a community which has been so tragically divided'. They were assured that Alliance 'offer determined and decisive leadership and the practical example of the community working together for the common good'.[2] Alliance fielded 34 candidates in the Assembly election; only eight were elected. Just over nine per cent of first-preference votes were cast for Alliance candidates, and it was only the proportional representation system, reintroduced after nearly fifty years, that gave Alliance a smattering of Assembly members. Not one Alliance candidate topped a constituency poll.

It was the Protestant working class who were the most hostile to Alliance. While Catholics were on the whole unwilling to give the party their first-preference vote, it did pick up a higher percentage of second-preference Catholic votes than second-preference Protestant votes. Alliance also received more first-preference support in Protestant middle-class areas than in working-class areas: 12·4 per cent of the vote in middle-class South Antrim compared with 6·6 per cent in working-class North Belfast.

The failure of Alliance to secure widespread Catholic support is readily understandable: any form of Unionism, no matter how pretty its face, is unacceptable. But how to explain the lack of votes from the Protestant side? Alliance was, after all, upholding and respecting the first principle of Protestant politics – the link with Britain – and so seemed to be making no great ideological break with the Unionist tradition. In fact they were. In reality, as previous chapters have shown, the Union with Britain has never been the guiding principle of either the upper-class leadership of Unionism or its lower-class followers. The first essential has always been what the Union protected: for the ruling establishment the undemocratic political control which preserved its economic and social ascendancy – the 'revolt of the business community', as Lord Londonderry put it;[3] and for the working-class Protestants, maintenance of the privileged position as a labour aristocracy. The Alliance Party offered Unionism without such guarantees and the Protestant community reacted accordingly. Bill Craig's form of Unionism, which he was then supporting – an independent Ulster, ascendancy without the Union – proved more attractive.

The popularity of Craig as compared with Alliance is not the only indication that ascendancy came before Union for the mass of Protestants. With the exception of the Alliance and NILP all the groups which stood in the Assembly election were to the right of Faulkner. By the following British general election of February 1974, the hardliners had advanced further; they captured all 11 Unionist seats and gained a majority against Faulknerism of approximately three to one in terms of votes cast, a figure that rose to five to one in October, in the second general election of the year.

Although the Protestant working class broke to the right, this did not necessarily rule out the emergence of more radical politics after the break: Tom Sloan of the Independent Orange Order originally criticised the Unionist establishment of being 'soft' on 'Romanism', and yet he, greatly assisted by Lindsay Crawford, adopted a more radical criticism of the Unionist ruling class.

Many people have looked for a similar movement within the post-1968 Protestant working class. In particular many on the English left have confidently predicted that in challenging the established leaders of the Unionist Party the Protestant working class would eventually be driven to adopting 'class politics'. At times there have been signs to encourage such an expectation. The names chosen for some of the recent Protestant groups are suggestive of a class approach; the Ulster Workers' Council is one, the Loyalist Association of Workers another. The UWC newspaper has carried articles on the indequacies of public transport, on how to claim social benefits and similar topics, suggesting that its emphasis is not exclusively sectarian. A number of individuals have had left-wing views attributed to them. Ernie 'Duke' Elliot, once a member of the UDA leadership, was said to 'walk around Woodvale with Che Guevara books stuffed in his pocket'.[4] He and other UDA notables like Tommy Heron and Dave Fogal have conducted talks with the Official IRA in an attempt to find common ground with Catholic workers. Even super-hero Gusty Spence said in a television interview after escaping from temporary parole:

> We have known squalor. I was born and reared in it. No one knows better than we do the meaning of slums, the meaning of deprivation, the meaning of suffering for what one believes in, whatever the ideology. In so far as people speak of fifty years of misrule I wouldn't disagree with that.[5]

Unfortunately for working-class unity it was not because he talked about slums and 'fifty years of misrule' that Gusty's name was painted on tenement walls. When Tommy Heron tried to gain political support in the Assembly election of 1973, as opposed to leading a paramilitary outfit, he received only 2,480 votes out of a possible 80,000-plus in the Protestant constituency of East Belfast; Tommy Lyttle, another UDA member, who had occasionally shown 'left-wing' leanings, did even worse, finishing last of 18 candidates in North Belfast. A more deadly judgement on both Heron and 'Duke' Elliot was their assassination by men from their own side; Elliot in December 1972 and Heron in September 1973, while Fogal fled to England where he spilt the beans to the *Sunday Times*. To put it bluntly, no grouping, as opposed to individuals, with left-wing tendencies has emerged from the Protestant community since 1968 and certainly there has been no resurrection of the unemployed unity of 1932, no renewal of the fragile working-class unity of 1905–1907. The UWC may carry articles on social benefits and use the general strike as a weapon, but it is, in the words of its constitution, 'solidly pledged to fight Irish republicanism and all forms of communism within the official trade-union movement and within the precinct of Ulster.'[6]

Nor has there been a break with the tradition of upper-class control in the parties which grew up out of dissatisfaction with the policies of O'Neill, Clark and Faulkner. The class composition of the leadership in the three main 'hardline' unionist parties at the 1975 Convention election – the official Unionists (by then led by Harry West), the DUP under Paisley, and the Vanguard Party under Craig – is indicated by the following table. The notable change from the old days is the absence of the landed aristocracy, but workers were outnumbered three to one even in Craig's Vanguard Party, which had the active support of the Loyalist Association of Workers at its formation. Paisley's party, although it contained the greatest social mix, had no 'leadership' to speak of as its candidates were Paisley's men and women, rather than those with an independent social position. The official Unionists were still very much the establishment party, and overall the political leadership of the Protestant community remains where it has always been – with money.

It is true that the ability of politicians to exercise control in

138

Northern Ireland is not what it was. The UWC strike of 1974 seems a case in point. The strike was initiated and organised throughout by the great mass of the Protestant community without their political leaders. Law and order were maintained, welfare work conducted, food collected and distributed, petrol rationed – society was organised either by the UWC, the UDA and UVF or by the many ad hoc street and district committees which sprang up as the strike spread. But although West, Paisley and Craig jumped on the bandwagon only when it became apparent that the strike had a chance of success, when the ordinary Protestant community promised to gain by their own unaided efforts the victory their leaders had been unable to achieve, they did manage to exert control over the political direction of the strike.

Normally the traditional leadership of the Protestant community has preferred to head off, rather than react to, independent Protestant working-class activity, by sponsoring such organisations (like the B Specials or the Unionist Labour

10.1 Occupation of Candidates in 1975 Convention Election

	UUC	DUP	UVP
businessman/company director	10	3	7
upper professional	7	0	4
lower professional	0	2	1
farmer	5	3	1
minister of religion	2	2	0
white-collar worker	1	0	2
foreman	0	1	0
blue-collar worker	0	1	2
politician	2	1	0
housewife	0	2	0
not stated	0	1	0

Data: from UUC, DUP and UVP

Association of old) which permit the activity but deny it independence. In the early 1970s the true heirs to such containment policies were Bill Craig and his Vanguard Party, into which were integrated the Loyalist Association of Workers and various paramilitary leaders like Glenn Barr of the UDA and three members of yet another paramilitary group, the Ulster Volunteer Service Corps, who stood as Vanguard candidates in the Convention election. Unfortunately for them, the inheritance turned out to be a shadow of what it was – Vanguard split asunder in October 1975 with Craig's conversion to power-sharing and Craig was outnumbered three to one by his own party members in the Convention.

Craig's conversion was tactical, but it was precisely because there was a tactical consensus that the Unionist alliance held together for as long as it did. The Protestant ruling class and the Protestant working class have always had different economic interests but they have also always shared a common tactic to maintain a status quo which suited them both – 'fenian-bashing'. From 1968 that agreement was no longer possible; the tactical consensus which had held together the Unionist alliance snapped, and the alliance disintegrated. No doubt the Unionist establishment would have been willing to go back on its 'reforms', but it could not retreat too far because of the spotlight the world had thrown on Northern Ireland and because the Catholic community would resist by all their means a return to the old days. 'Ulster is at the crossroads', Terence O'Neill once said, but the problem for the rulers of Northern Ireland was that whichever road was taken was either barricaded by the loyalists or mined by the republicans.

The dilemma resulted in the multiplicity of political parties within Unionism, separated at times by class interests – the upper-class Unionist Party, the petty-bourgeois DUP – but more often by tactical disagreements: whether to ban this or that march, to introduce internment, to disband the B Specials, to adopt power-sharing, opt for an independent Ulster or full integration into Westminster or a Stormont with reduced powers.

On some occasions the disintegration was reflected in the paramilitaries. When Craig came out in favour of temporary power-sharing, the leadership of the UDA, one of the two main organisations, supported him; but the other, the UVF, took Paisley's side. Usually, however, the squabbles amongst the paramilitaries are even less political. The Ulster Freedom Fighters, for example, came into existence when the UDA was in one of its more passive moods, and the group announced its arrival by a series of sectarian assassinations. Even the regular killing of Catholics is not enough for some groups. One of them, 'Tara', believes in eliminating all Catholics within the Ulster state and even dreams of eventually taking over the south. There are differences in structure, the UDA aiming at a mass membership, the UVF not, but what they all hold in common is a near absence of economic and social policies, of what is normally considered to be the substance of policies.

The lack of any real political differences between the working-class Protestant groups is not surprising. All the poems, songs and jokes quoted in this book have reflected the thorough-going reactionary nature of that class's political consciousness. Assassinations of Catholics because they are Catholics, the bombing without warning of Catholic pubs because they are owned by Catholics, are not foreign to the Protestant community, because they are not foreign to that community's culture. To ignore that culture is to court political insignificance. The Alliance Party ignored it with the consequences described above. But so have many well to the left of the Alliance Party.

The Northern Ireland situation has a particular relevance to the marxist left because the state has suffered the type of political crisis marxists dream of – barricades in the streets, large sections of the population engaged in armed struggle against the state, communities running themselves, and what seemed to be a colonial situation straight out of the nineteenth century. But since the growth of the Provisionals, marxists, in Britain especially, have lost a good deal of their enthusiasm for the 'Irish struggle'. The

141

spectacle of worker fighting worker does not readily fit into the traditional marxist scheme of workers uniting to overthrow capitalism. Not surprisingly, all manner of explanations have been offered for the non-arrival of the millennium, the most important being that the Protestant workers are the victims of years of anti-Catholic propaganda. On this view, what is needed above all is for the Protestants to be 'educated' through concentrating on social and economic questions and so achieving some measure of Protestant–Catholic unity in practice; the national question should be relegated until such time as the Protestant workers have learned to trust their Catholic counterparts. Alternatively it is proposed that with the worsening of the capitalist crisis, a natural unity will be forged between the two sections of the working class because the marginal privileges of one of them will become irrelevant.

Unfortunately, it is not enough to say that the Protestant workers have been brainwashed by a cunning upper-class leadership, that all can be changed by soapbox oratory or the selling of socialist newspapers outside the Belfast shipyards. The skilled and unskilled labourer in England may be able to unite in pressing economic demands, but the material differences between them are not as great or as inherited as in Northern Ireland; and they do not support different football teams, tell different jokes, go to different clubs, belong to different sections of the trade-union movement. They do not have opposing views on the right of the state to exist. It may be good textbook marxism to say that Protestant and Catholic workers will unite once they suffer equally, but that has never happened to any great extent before and the reason it has never happened, and is unlikely to happen, is that the two sections of the working class have not suffered equally; while the Orange state exists, there is no evidence that they will. While there are some Protestant jobs at Sorocco, if only a few hundred, while there are Protestant jobs at the shipyards, if only a few thousand, those jobs will be there while the Catholic jobs will not.

The view that the Protestant working class are merely deluded workers has a counterpart in the Provisionals' often

142

expressed view of the Protestants as deluded Irishmen who will come to their good Irish senses in time. The Provisionals often make endearing little pleas to the Protestants:

> The Provisionals ask the majority in the North to unite with them in making a new nation, an old country. Six counties is but a fraction of Ireland; the Protestant and Presbyterian peoples of the North have as much birthright to the twenty-six as have any Catholic. It is our dearest wish that they would claim that birthright now and having claimed it that they then proceed to enrich and cultivate it with the industry for which they are renowned.[7]

These words were not meant to be as patronising as they sound, but they show a severe lack of realism in expecting the Protestants to forgive the bombing of their Ulster, the killing of their policemen, the murder of members of their community in the Ulster Defence Regiment. In practice the Provisionals have not concerned themselves overmuch with winning the Protestants to their cause and certainly they have not gone the way of the Official IRA and identified assassination targets in their own community to Protestant militants. In practice the Provisionals' attitude towards militant loyalists is rather less compassionate than the call for unity would suggest. As an article on the UFF, then the leading assassination outfit put it in the Provisional newspaper in 1973, 'THIS UGLY CREATURE MUST BE DESTROYED'.[8]

Not a very pleasant conclusion, but an understandable one at the time, given the campaign of sectarian assassinations against Catholics. As understandable as are the reactions of the Northern Ireland Protestants. It is only to be expected that they wish to maintain the Protestant ascendancy. The settlers cannot be blamed for wanting to hold what they have against the intrusions of the unwashed natives. But neither can the working-class settlers be judged innocent, as if none of it was at their making, as if they were a neutral force in history, pushed and prodded without their compliance. Of course they are not the key villains. Those who have whipped up the sectarianism, have grown fat on it, have bought country houses on it, they, or, more pointedly, the economic and social system they represent, are the untouchables. But the working-class Protestants are not innocent.

In that at least they are not alone. But alone in most other ways they now are. If the Protestant working class have learnt one thing from 1968–75 it is that apart from a few friends in the British military machine they have no friends left. Their former sponsors, the British ruling class, have deserted them; the Northern Ireland gentry and factory-owners want them to be quiet; even Bill Craig, who had stood by them for so long, finally found them an embarrassment. Their trust in their leaders, their faith in British imperialism, have finally caught up with them.

Well may the Protestant workers protest that they are being badly rewarded by the Harold Wilsons and Ted Heaths for all their years of loyal service to that imperialism. Right they are to remind the English ruling class that over 5,000 Ulster working-class Protestants died in the Battle of the Somme so that Britain could gain a few more inches of land. The anniversary of that battle is another occasion when Orangemen march through the towns of Northern Ireland, quoting the words of Sir William Spencer: 'I am not an Ulsterman but yesterday the 1st of July as I followed their amazing attack on the Somme I felt I would rather be an Ulsterman than anything else in the world.' The words are quoted with pride, they are woven into Orange banners, the Orange Order distributes a booklet entitled 'Rather Be an Ulsterman'. Such is the tragedy of the ordinary Ulster Protestant, if Ulster be the adjective they prefer. They quote the words not with anger at the senseless carnage, at the way they were sacrificed so that well-fed, high-living Englishmen could enjoy themselves for a few more years. They are not bitter at the slaughter of their own people in one of the most pointless military battles the world had ever seen, a battle judged necessary at the time by those not of their class, not of their country. They are not angry, they are not bitter, they do not protest; they are proud.

That is their tragedy.

References

1. 'This We Will Maintain'

1. Ulster Defence Association, *Detainee Song Book 1974*, Belfast: UDA 1974.
2. *Orange Cross*, Belfast, no.20.
3. *ibid.* February 1972.
4. Ulster Unionist Party, *27 Myths About Ulster*, Belfast: UUP 1972.
5. *Orange Loyalist Songs 1971*, Belfast: 1971, p.15.
6. Ulster Vanguard Party, *Ulster, A Nation*, Belfast: UVP 1972.
7. A.T.Q.Stewart, *The Ulster Crisis*, London: Faber 1969, p.80.
8. R.McNeill, *Ulster's Stand For Union*, London: John Murray 1922, p.279.
9. *Crimson Banner Song Book*, Belfast: 1975, p.64.
10. The Sunday Times Insight Team, *Ulster*, London: Penguin 1972, p.213.
11. *Loyalist News*, 30 September 1972.
12. L.P.Curtis, *Coercion and Conciliation in Ireland*, Princeton: Princeton University Press 1963, p.33.
13. D.Gwynn, *The History of Partition*, Dublin: Browne & Nolan 1950, p.46.
14. *Crimson Banner Song Book*, *op. cit.* p.80.
15. *Irish Times, Annual Review 1972*, Dublin: Irish Times 1972, p.7.
16. Ulster Vanguard Party, *op. cit.* p.10.
17. *ibid.* p.11.
18. Press statement issued by a Protestant paramilitary group, believed to be the Ulster Volunteer Force. M.Dillon and D.Lehane, *Political Murder in Northern Ireland*, London: Penguin 1973, p.281.
19. *Crimson Banner Song Book*, *op. cit.* p.63.

2. Ancient Privileges

1. H.Senior, *Orangeism in Ireland and Britain*, London: Routledge & Kegan Paul 1966, p.6.
2. J.W.Boyle, *The Rise of the Irish Labour Movement*, unpublished thesis, p.76.
3. *ibid.* p.113.
4. *Belfast News-Letter*, 30 April 1914.
5. J.C.Beckett and R.E.Glasscock, *Belfast*, London: British Broadcasting Corporation 1967, p. 148.
6. *ibid.* p.148.
7. *Northern Ireland Development Programme 1970*, Belfast: HMSO 1970, p.104.
8. Department of Finance, *Social and Economic Trends in Northern Ireland*, Belfast: HMSO 1975, p.17.
9. Central Register Office, *Census of Population, 1961*, Belfast 1961–65.
10. *Northern Ireland Development Programme, op. cit.* p.104.
11. *ibid.* p.104.
12. Ulster Unionist Council, *Ulster Change and Progress*, Belfast: UUC 1970.
13. *Northern Ireland Development Programme, op. cit.* p.104.
14. Department of Finance, *op. cit.* p.47.
15. *Disturbances in Northern Ireland* (Cameron Report) HMSO 1969.
16. *Belfast News-Letter*, 30 April 1914.

3. Leaders of the Cause

1. S.J.Ervine, *Craigavon – Ulsterman*, London: Allen & Unwin 1949, p.185.
2. H.M.Hyde, *Lord Carson*, London: Heinemann 1953, p.100.
3. *Northern Ireland Hansard*, vol.5, col.1281.
4. J.C.Beckett, *The Making of Modern Ireland*, London: Faber 1966, p.425.
5. *Belfast News-Letter*, 10 December 1918.

6. F.McManus (ed.), *The Years of the Great Test*, Cork: Mercier 1967, p.147.

7. *Northern Whig*, 15 October 1920.

8. G.C.Duggan, *Northern Ireland – success or failure?* Dublin: Irish Times, 1950, p.21.

9. *Northern Ireland Hansard,* vol.7, col.17.

10. *ibid.* vol.16, col.1091.

11. *ibid.* vol.16, col.1070.

12. *Protestant Telegraph*, 3 August 1968.

13. *ibid.* 27 August 1966.

14. *ibid.* 21 January 1967.

15. *ibid.* 4 January 1967.

16. *ibid.* 14 December 1968.

17. *ibid.* 22 June 1968.

18. *ibid.* 3 February 1968.

19. *ibid.* 4 February 1967.

20. *ibid.* 28 October 1968.

21. *ibid.* 19 November 1968.

22. *ibid.* 4 January 1967.

23. *ibid.* 10 August 1968.

24. *ibid.* 30 November 1966.

25. *ibid.* 22 March 1969.

26. *Time Out*, issue 124, 30 June–6 July 1972.

27. *Irish Times*, 27 November 1971.

28. *Protestant Telegraph*, 1 December 1971.

4. The Protestant Way of Life

1. This and the following, Geoffrey Bell, 'A Day in the Life of a Linfield Fan', *Irish Times*, 4 February 1971.

2. *Orange Loyalist Songs 1971*, Belfast: 1971, p.34.

3. *Belfast Telegraph*, 10 May 1969.

4. *Loyalist News*, 20 March 1971.

5. *ibid.* 13 August 1974.

6. *Ulster Loyalist*, 4 June 1974.

7. *Orange Cross*, no.78.

8. Ulster Defence Association, *Detainee Song Book 1974*, Belfast: UDA 1974.

9. *ibid.*

10. *Orange Loyalist Songs, op. cit.* p.8.

11. *ibid.* p. 28.

12. *Orange Cross*, no.21.

13. *Loyalist News*, 8 April 1972.

14. *Crimson Banner Song Book*, Belfast: 1975, p.103.

15. Ulster Defence Association, *op. cit.*

16. Interview: author with Tommy Lyttle, June 1975.

17. Interview: author with Walter Williams, Imperial General Secretary, Orange Order, June 1975.

18. M.W.Dewar, J.Brown and S.E.Long, *Orangeism: A New Historical Appreciation*, Belfast: Grand Orange Lodge of Ireland 1967, p.104.

19. *Crimson Banner Song Book, op. cit.* p.97.

20. Independent Television Authority, *Religion in Northern Ireland*, Belfast: ITA 1969, p.3.

21.*Combat*, no.21.

22. *WDA News*, no.17.

23. *Crimson Banner Song Book, op. cit.* p.8.

24. *The United Ulsterman*, January 1975.

25. *Crimson Banner Song Book, op. cit.* p.25.

26. Geoffrey Bell, 'Schooling, Northern Style', *Irish Times*, 30 December 1970.

27. *UWC Journal*, vol.1, no.2.

5. Lundies

1. *Belfast News-Letter*, 28 November 1918.

2. *ibid.* 22 May 1929.

3. *ibid.* 26 January 1949.

4. J.D.Clarkson, *Labour and Nationalism in Ireland*, New York: Columbia University Press 1925, p.374.

5. *Belfast News-Letter*, 10 December 1918.

6. *ibid.* 26 January 1932.

7. *ibid.* 11 May 1921.

8. Ulster Unionist Council, *Annual Report 1974*, Belfast: UUC 1974, p.17.

9. J.W.Good, *Ulster and Ireland*, Dublin: Maunsel, 1919, p.76.

10. *Belfast News-Letter*, 6 January 1910.

11. *ibid.* 6 December 1918.

12. *ibid.* 21 January 1938.

13. *ibid.* 27 April 1923.

14. *ibid.* 30 November 1923.

15. The details of this campaign have been taken from contemporary newspaper reports in *Belfast News-Letter*.

16. W.Walker, 'Rebel Ireland', in Cork Workers' Club, *The Connolly/Walker Controversy*, Cork: Cork Workers' Club 1974, p.5.

17. *ibid.* p.2.

18. *ibid.* p.16.

19. *ibid.* p.5.

20. *Irish Protestant*, 9 September 1905.

21. Cork Workers' Club, *op. cit.* p.3.

22. *ibid.* p.5.

23. *Irish Protestant*, 1 April 1905.

24. *ibid.* 24 June 1905.

25. J.W.Boyle, 'The Belfast Protestant Association and the Independent Orange Order', *Irish Historical Studies*, no.13, p.127.

26. *ibid.* p.135.

27. *Irish Protestant*, 25 February 1905.

28. *ibid.* 4 March 1905.

29. *ibid.*

30. J.W.Boyle, *The Rise of the Irish Labour Movement*, unpublished thesis, p.284.

31. *Irish Protestant*, 11 March 1905.

32. *ibid.* 20 May 1905.

33. *ibid.* 31 March 1906.

34. *ibid.* 7 January 1905.

6. The Workers

1. *Northern Whig*, 4 May 1926.
2. *Irish Times*, 6 May 1926.
3. *ibid*. 13 May 1926.
4. Emmet Larkin, *James Larkin*, London: Routledge & Kegan Paul 1965, p.26.
5. James Connolly, *Ireland upon the Dissecting Table* (1913), Cork: Cork Workers' Club 1974, p.35.
6. Samuel Levenson, *James Connolly*, London: Martin Brian & O'Keefe, 1973, p.221.
7. *Guardian*, 14 February 1973.
8. *Northern Ireland Statistical Abstract 1974*, Belfast: HMSO, 1975.
9. Department of Finance, Northern Ireland, *Social and Economic Trends in Northern Ireland*, Belfast: HMSO 1975, p.13.
10. *Belfast News-Letter*, 12 July 1963.
11. R.J.Babbington MP, quoted in *Time Out*, issue 124, 30 June–6 July 1972.
12. Interview conducted by author with Tommy Lyttle, June 1975.
13. Orange Order, *The Twelfth 1975*, Belfast: Orange Order 1975, p.15.
14. K.I.Simms, 'Government and trade unions – the situation in Northern Ireland', *British Journal of Industrial Relations*, vol.2, 1964, p.260.
15. Andrew Boyd, *The Rise of Irish Trade Unions*, Dublin: Anvil 1970, appendix.
16. Irish Congress of Trade Unions, *Trade Union Information*, Dublin: ICTU 1972. The discrepancy in figures is made up by Northern Ireland-based unions.

7. The Bosses

1. *Crimson Banner Song Book*, Belfast 1975, p.31.
2. A.T.Q.Stewart, *The Ulster Crisis*, London: Faber 1969, p.77.
3. *The Times*, 9 May 1913.
4. Irish Loyal and Patriotic Union, *Pamphlets*, Dublin: ILPU 1888.

5. *ibid.*

6. Irish Unionist Alliance, *The Case Against Home Rule*, Dublin: IUA 1907, p.33.

7. *ibid.* p.72.

8. Various writers, *Against Home Rule*, Dublin 1912, p.38.

9. *Belfast News-Letter*, 16 May 1870.

10. D.Thornley, *Isaac Butt*, London: McGibbon & Kee 1964, p.87.

11. E.Strauss, *Irish Nationalism and British Democracy*, London, Methuen 1951, p.189.

12. Ulster Vanguard Party, *Ulster, A Nation*, Belfast: UVP 1972, pp.9–10.

13. *Ulster Year Book*, Belfast: HMSO 1926.

14. N.Mansergh, *Government of Northern Ireland*, London: Allen & Unwin 1949, p.86.

15. *Belfast News-Letter*, 13 July 1927.

16. *Northern Ireland Hansard*, vol.10, col.28.

17. *Belfast News-Letter*, 21 May 1929.

18. *ibid.* 22 May 1919.

19. *ibid.* 5 October 1932.

20. *ibid.* 7 October 1932.

21. J.J.Kelly, 'A journalist's diary', *Capuchin Annual*, 1944.

22. *Belfast News-Letter*, 15 October 1932.

23. *ibid.* 13 October 1932.

24. *ibid.* 13 July 1933.

25. The seats were: Oldpark, Pottinger, Shankill, St Anné's, Woodvale, and the mixed Catholic/Protestant area of Dock. Figures based on data from contemporary newspapers.

26. J.J.Kelly, *op. cit.*

27. *Belfast News-Letter*, 23 July 1935.

28. *ibid.* 19 July 1959.

29. *ibid.* 13 July 1960.

8. The Fenians

1. *Northern Ireland Hansard*, vol.83, col.1058.

2. *Nusight*, November 1969.

3. *ibid.* November 1969.

4. *Economic and Social Review* (Dublin), January 1972.

5. *Nusight*, November 1969.

6. Government Publication Office, Dublin, *Dáil Éireann Parliamentary Debates*, vol.138.

7. *Irish Times*, 12 April 1951.

8. T.Kettle, *The Open Secret of Ireland*, London: W.J.Ham-Smith, 1912, p.115.

9. L.P.Curtis, *Coercion and Conciliation in Ireland*, Princeton: Princeton University Press 1963, p.5.

10. E.Strauss, *Irish Nationalism and British Democracy*, London: Methuen 1951, p.137.

11. N.D.Palmer, *The Irish Land League Crisis*, New Haven: Yale University Press 1940, p.288.

12. M.Davitt, 'History of the Land League', in D.B.Cashman, *The Life of Michael Davitt*, Glasgow: Cameron and Ferguson, 1882, p.221.

13. Letter in Belfast Public Records Office, D.1481.

14. C.C.O'Brien, *Parnell and His Party*, Oxford: Clarendon Press 1957, p.130.

15. Michael Davitt, *The Fall of Feudalism in Ireland*, London: Harper 1904, p.377.

16. Emmet Larkin, *James Larkin*, London: Routledge & Kegan Paul 1965, p.34.

17. James Connolly, *Ireland upon the Dissecting Table* (1913), Cork: Cork Workers' Club 1974, p.47.

18. James Connolly, *Selected Writings* (ed. B.Ellis), London: Penguin 1973, p.283.

19. McCann has his own lengthy critique in, Eamonn McCann, *War and an Irish Town*, London: Penguin 1974.

20. *Irish Times*, 21 January 1969.

21. *Resistance*, August 1969. 'Official' in this context was the then leadership of Sinn Fein/IRA, which had not yet split into Official and Provisional. These leaders all remained Officials after the split.

9. Protestantism's Last Stand

1. *Orange Loyalist Songs 1971*, Belfast: 1971, p.23.
2. See chapter 7, p.101.
3. The Sunday Times Insight Team, *Ulster*, London: Penguin 1972, p.206.
4. *Protestant Telegraph*, 30 March 1968.
5. *Belfast Telegraph*, 4 August 1971.
6. *Belfast News-Letter*, 12 October 1968.
7. *ibid.* 16 October 1968.
8. *ibid.* 23 October 1968.
9. *Belfast Telegraph*, 3 August 1971.
10. *ibid.* 19 August 1971.
11. *ibid.* 12 April 1972.
12. *ibid.* 5 April 1972.
13. *Belfast News-Letter*, 8 January 1973.
14. *Belfast Telegraph*, 30 August 1972.
15. *ibid.*
16. *ibid.* 5 April 1972.
17. See M.Dillon and D.Lehane, *Political Murder in Northern Ireland*, London: Penguin 1973.
18. *Loyalist News*, 17 February 1973.
19. *ibid.* 20 September 1972.
20. *ibid.* 2 September 1972.
21. *ibid.* 30 September 1972.
22. *UWC Journal*, vol.1, no.2.

10. 'O God our help in ages past, Our hope for years to come'

1. Orange Order, *The Twelfth 1975*, Belfast: Orange Order 1975, p.25.
2. Alliance Party, *Election Manifesto, Assembly 1973*, Belfast: Alliance Party 1973.
3. See chapter 7, p.99.

4. M.Dillon and D.Lehane, *Political Murder in Northern Ireland*, London: Penguin 1973, p.171.

5. *ibid.*

6. *UWC Journal*, vol.1, no.2.

7. Provisional IRA, *Freedom Struggle*, Dublin: IRA 1973.

8. *Republican News*, 30 June 1973.

Index

Act of Union, 16,98

Alliance Party, 130,134–6,141

Amalgamated Society of Engineers, 85

Amalgamated Transport and General Workers Union, 86

Ancient Order of Hibernians, 113

Andersonstown, 53

Andrews, Irene, 128

Andrews, John, 40,41,67

Anglo-Irish Free Trade Agreement, 123

Antrim, 15,21

Apprentice Boys, 53,121

Armagh, 21,28,30,32,46,111

Baldwin, Stanley, 24

Ballot Act, 55

Ballymena, 31,42

Battle of the Somme, 144

Belfast, 3,8,9,10,38,49,51,56,71,96, 111,115,119,133,138; Celtic Football Club, 48; Chamber of Commerce, 95,97,100; Corporation, 71,73,74,109; economic and social conditions, 16–30; labour movement, 71, 73–4,113; Trades Council, 72,75, 81,83,85; trade unionism, 66, 80–6

Belfast News-Letter, 69,97,98, 102,103,124

Belfast Telegraph, 123,124,125, 126,134

Bible Standards League, 67

Birth control, 109,117

Bleakley, David, 72,133

'Bloody Sunday', 1–3,5,9,122,125

Boilermakers' Union, 85

Bombay Street, Belfast, 52

Boyd, Alexander, 82,113

British Army, 1,2,3,11,115,121

British and Irish Communist Organisation, 13,14

Brooke, Basil (Lord Brookeborough), 40,41,45,46,65, 104

B Specials, 39,48,121,124,127,139, 140

Buller, Charles Dunbar, 75

Burroughs, Ronald, 121

Burntollet Bridge, 127

Butt, Isaac, 97

Calvinism, 44,46,59–60,107

Carson, Edward, (Lord Carson), 34–8,40,41,46,47,65,67,71,94, 95,98,120,133

Carters' Association, 82

Cavan, 7

Censorship, 109

Churches' Industrial Council, 90

Church of Ireland, 62

Churchill, Randolph, 9

Civil Rights Association, 117

Civil Rights movement, 1,42,46,87, 92,108,110,114,115,116,117,134

Clanricord, Lord, 37

Clark, James Chichester, 41,121–2, 138

Clark, George, 94

Clifton, 29

Clow, W.M. 69

Communism, 43,104,138

Connolly, James, 73–4,83–5,110, 113,114,116,117

Constitution of the Irish Republic, 45,110
Cooper, Bob, 135
Cooper, Ivan, 115
Corish, Brendan, 109
Cork, 17
Cosgrave, Liam, 14
Council of Ireland, 5,81
Court, 28,29
Craig, C.C. 69
Craig, James (Lord Craigavon), 36, 38,40,41,45,46,47,65,94,100–1, 109,114,133
Craig, William, 11,60,99,107,131, 135,136,138,139,140,141,144
Craigavon, 38
Crawford, Lindsay, 74–9,82,137
Cromac, 29
Cushendon, Lord, 7

Davison, Joseph, 70
Davitt, Michael, 76,110–13
Democratic Unionist, 66
Democratic Unionist Party, 45, 131,134,140
Devlin, Bernadette, 115
Devlin, Joe, 82,83,101,110, 113–14,116,117
Divorce, 110,117
Dixon, Captain, 102
Dock, 29,30
Donegal, 7,111
Down, 15,21
Drogheda, 81
Dublin, 73,75,81,90; Chamber of Commerce, 95; economic and social conditions, 17,19,23,108; Lock-Out (1913), 113
Duggan, G.C. 39
Duncairn, 29
Dungannon, 32
Dunleath, Lord, 94
Dupont, 123

Edinburgh, Duke of, 41
Education, 60–2
Elliot, Ernie, 'Duke', 137–8

Enniskillen, 111
Evening News, 37
Evicted Tenants' Commission, 37

Falls, Belfast, 2,25,26,27,28,29,30, 103
Faulkner, Brian, 14,41,44–5,72,87, 105, 106–7,130,133,136,138
Federation of Engineering and Shipping Trades, 85
Fermanagh, 32
Fitt, Gerry, 109
Fogal, Dave, 137–8
Free Presbyterian Church, 42

Gaelic League, 77
Galway, 17
Galway, Mary, 85
General Strike (1926), 80–1,89
Gladstone, William, 98
Glasgow Rangers, 48,49
Grant, William, 67

Heath, Edward, 144
Henderson, Tom, 70–1,102
Heron, Tommy, 137–8
Home Government Association, 97
Home Rule, 6,23,68,77,78,83,95, 98,99,113,114
Home Rule crisis (1912–14), 6,23, 35,36,94
Home Rule movement, 97
Hüll, Billy, 92
Hume, John, 51,115–16

ICI, 123
Illiteracy, 20–1
Independent Labour Party, 66,73, 74
Independent Loyalist, 134
Independent Orange Order, 75–6, 78,137
Independent Pro-White Paper, 134
Independent Unionists, 66,68–71, 75,76,100–1,102,104,134
Industrial Relations Act, 92

Internment, 1,45,92,106,122,124, 125,127,130
Irish Congress of Trade Unions, 81,89–91,92; Northern Ireland Committee, 89–91,92; *see also* Irish Trade Union Congress
Irish Labour Party, 14,109
Irish National Teachers' Organisation, 91
Irish Protestant, 75,76,77,78
Irish Republican Army, 50,51,55, 105,106,107,124,125,129; 'Officials', 116–17,128,137,143; 'Provisionals', 5,14,117,121,122, 125,127,128,134,141,142–3
Irish Republican Socialist Party, 117,128
Irish Trade Union Congress,72,89; *see also* Irish Congress of Trade Unions
Irish Transport and General Workers' Union, 83–5,91
Irish Unionist Alliance, 96

James II, 65
Jameson Raid, 37

Kane, R. 56
Keady, 30
Kennedy, John F. 43
Krushchev, Nikita, 13
Kyle, Sam, 80

'Labour Aristocracy', 17–33
Labour movement, 65,66,71–4
Labour Party (British), 39
Labour Representation Committee, 66
Ladies Orange Association, 55
Lake, General, 15–16
Land Acts: (1881), 112; (1885), 68; (1903), 68
Land League, 111–12
Land question, 16,111
Land war, 56,111–12
Larkin, James, 82–3,84,110, 113–14

Larne, 31; Aluminium strike, 84
Law, A.Bonar, 9
Lemass, Sean, 44,122,123
Liberal Party, 35,37,76,83,99,135
Limerick, 17
Linfield Football Club, 48–9,58,60
Lloyd George, David, 6
Londonderry, 1,2,3,53,64,65,81,86, 114,124; Corporation, 32,48; Economic and social conditions, 1, 27,31
Londonderry, Lord, 94,96,99,136
Long Kesh, 54
Lonsdale, James, 134
Loyalist Party, 134
Loyalist Association of Workers, 92, 137,138,140
Loyalist News, 128
'Lundies', 64–79
Lundy, Robert, 65
Lurgan, 31,112
Lyttle, Tommy, 89,90,138

MacAteer, Eddie, 110,114,116
McCann, Eamonn, 115,116
MacDonald, Ramsay, 32
McKeague, John, 9
Maghermore Manifesto, 76,78
Manufacturers Act (1964), 123
Marxism, 4,43,83,89,111–12
Maudling, Reginald, 1,8
Midgley, Harry,72
Mill, John Stuart, 111
Monaghan, 7,21
Moorman, John, 42
'Motiveless Murders', 127–8

National Front, 4
National Front Loyalist, 134
National League, 112
National Union of Dock Labourers, 82
National Union of Teachers, 91
Nationalist Party, 105,110,113,114
New Ulster Movement, 134–5
'New Unionism', 81–3
Newry, 31

Northern Ireland Assembly, 34,122, 134,135,136,137
Northern Ireland Convention, 34, 72, 138, 139, 140
Northern Ireland Labour Party, 66 71,72,74,92,133,134,135,136

O'Brien, Conor Cruise, 14
O'Brien, William, 84
Ogilby, Anne, 55
Omagh, 32
O'Neill, Terence, 31,38,41,44,50, 66,92,121,122,134,135,138,140
Orange Order, 45,53,55—8,68,70, 75,87,88,89,104,105,111,132,144
Ormeau, 29

Paisley, Eileen, 109
Paisley, Ian, 41—7,55,58,77,107, 122,126,131,135,138,139,141
Parnell, Charles, 110—13,117
Partition, origins of, 5—7
People's Democracy, 115,116,127
Plantation of Ulster, 7—8
Powell, Enoch, 4,67
Presbyterians, 15,16,63,143
Press, British, 3,53
Progressive Unionist, 60,69
Proportional Representation, 100—1,102,135
Protestant Action, 131
Protestant Telegraph, 41,43,46,77
Pottinger, 29,30

Queens University Belfast, 101

Railway Clerks' Association, 80
Ravenhill, 58
Red Hand Commandos, 131
Redmond, John, 110,113,114,117
Richardson, George Reilly, 94,97
Roberts, Field Marshal, 94
Royal Irish Constabulary, 82
Royal Ulster Constabulary, 110, 124,127
Russell, T. W. 68—9

Saint Anne's, 25,29
Saint George's, 25,29
Salisbury, Lord, 9
Sandy Row, 52,103
Second International, 83
Shankill, 25,26,27,28,29,30,49,71, 103,119,121,130; Defence Association, 89
Sinn Fein, 71,104
Sloan, Tom, 75—8,82—3,113,137
Smithfield, 25,29
Social Democratic and Labour Party, 107,109,116,122,128,131
Soper, Donald, 42
Special Powers Act, 116
Spence, 'Gusty', 119—20,122,127, 137
Spencer, William, 144
Stalin, Joseph, 4,13
Stewart, W.J. 69—70
Straban, 31
Sunday Times, 138
Sunningdale Agreement, 5

Tandragee, 30
Tara, 131,141
Textile Operatives Society, 85
Times, 95
Tories, 9,10,36,37,56,76,97,98
Trades Disputes Act (1900), 37
Trades Disputes and Trade Union Act (1927), 89
Trades Union Congress, 5,81,90
Trade unionism, 23,80—92
Trinity College Dublin, 36
'Two Nations' Theory, 4,13—14
Tyrone, 21,32

Ulster Citizen Army, 131
Ulster Constitutional Loyalist, 134
Ulster Covenant, 5
'Ulster Custom', 16
Ulster Defence Association, 3,51, 55,129,137,138,139,140,141
Ulster Defence Regiment, 143
Ulster Freedom Fighters, 131,141, 143

Ulster Irish League, 96
Ulster Liberal Unionist Association, 96
Ulster Protestant League, 104
Ulster Special Constabulary, 56
Ulster Unionist Council, 55,67,131
Ulster Unionist Labour Association, 66–8,139–40
Ulster Unionist Party, 3,10–11, 34–5,40,41,45,55,65–8,88,96, 100–2,105,106–7,114,122,131, 134,137,138–9,140
Ulster Volunteer Force (1912–14), 23,56,94
Ulster Volunteer Force (1966–76), 46,51,59,117,119,131,139,141
Ulster Volunteer Service Corps, 131, 140
Ulster Workers' Council, 13,130, 137,138,139; General Strike, 4–5, 11,45,81,122,130,139
Unemployment, 1,10,24–6,87
Unemployment Relief Riots (1932), 102–4
Unionism, 14,35–6,38,39,40,41,56, 69,70,72,75,88,97,98,120,123, 125,136,140
Unionists, 6–7,21,27,31,35,65,68, 70,72,75,88,98–9,135
Unionist Anti-White Paper, 134

United Irishmen, 15–16, 55

Vance, Cecil, 86
Vanguard Party, 11–12,60,99,131, 134,137,138,139,140
Vietnam War, 43
Victoria, 29,30

Wage rates, 17–20
Walker, William, 71,72–4,75,77,80, 90
Wallace, R.H. 94
Ward, Peter, 119
Waterford, 17
West, Harry, 138,139
Wilde, Oscar, 37
William III, 65
Wilson, Harold, 4,8,11,14,144
Wilson, Havelock, 37
Wilson, Paddy, 128
Windsor, 29
Women, Protestant view of, 53–5
'Women Together', 53
Woods, P.J. 70
Woodvale, 29,137; Defence Association, 59
World Cup (1958), 133

Young, Arthur, 121
Young Unionist Association, 135

Michael Farrell

Northern Ireland: the Orange State

The first full-length political history of Northern Ireland. It describes the bloody pogroms with which the Unionist leaders, armed and financed by Britain, established their state; how they created an Orange state based on Protestant privilege. It records how in every decade the Catholics have been driven to armed revolt, and the few great moments of working-class solidarity. Michael Farrell traces the recent development of Loyalism into a threat to the traditional power structure in Northern Ireland.

Available from
Pluto Press
Unit 10 Spencer Court, 7 Chalcot Road,
London NW1 8LH

Complete list of
Pluto books and pamphlets
available on request